The Pepper Garden

Also by Dave DeWitt

Hot Spots
Chile Peppers: A Selected Bibliography of the Capsicums
Texas Monthly Guide to New Mexico

WITH NANCY GERLACH
The Fiery Cuisines
Fiery Appetizers
The Whole Chile Pepper Book
Just North of the Border

WITH MARY JANE WILAN
The Food Lover's Handbook to the Southwest

Also by Paul W. Bosland

Capsicum: A Comprehensive Bibliography

WITH ALTON BAILEY AND DONALD COTTER
Growing Chiles in New Mexico

WITH ALTON BAILEY AND
JAIME IGLESIAS-OLIVAS
Pepper Varieties and Classification

The
Pepper
Garden

Dave DeWitt & Paul W. Bosland

Ten Speed Press
Berkeley, California

1⊖
TEN SPEED PRESS
P.O. Box 7123
Berkeley, CA 94707

Text and cover design by Nancy Austin
Cover photo by Paul W. Bosland

PHOTOGRAPHS

Paul W. Bosland: pages 170, 194
Dave Dewitt: pages 8, 36, 45, 60, 65, 114, 123, 139, 142, 148, 154, 158,
    168, 174, 184, 198, 203, 207, 208
Victor Espinosa: pages 25, 27, 29, 31, 32, 38, 39, 41, 46, 48, 50, 51, 53,
    55, 56, 64, 68, 181
Jaime Iglesias-Olivas: page 6

Library of Congress Cataloging-in-Publication Data
DeWitt, Dave.
    The pepper garden / Dave DeWitt and Paul W.
    Bosland.
        p.   cm.
    Includes bibliographical references (p.   ) and index.
    ISBN 0-89815-554-1
    1. Peppers.   I. Bosland, Paul W.   II. Title.
    SB351.P4D47   1993
    633.8′4—dc20   93-30508
                                                  CIP

FIRST PRINTING 1993

Printed in the United States of America

        4   5   —   97   96   95

To the memory of Fabian Garcia,
the plant breeder who originated the modern
New Mexican chile pepper varieties
in the early 1900s

CONTENTS

ACKNOWLEDGMENTS

Thanks to all the enthusiastic pepper growers and aficionados who helped with this book:

Alton Bailey, Chel Beeson, Judy Bosland, William Burke, Jeff Campbell, Diane Chamberlain, Beverly Dayton, Jo Ann Deck, Cal Dennler, Victor Espinosa, Howard Essl, Jeff and Nancy Gerlach, John Graham, Daphne Gould, Cecilia Height, Gene Henderson, Antonio Heras-Duran, Annette Hill, Laurent Hodges, Dick Horst, Stuart and Elizabeth Hutson, Pat Kiewicz, Graham Jacks, Ellen Jacobson, Stuart Jeffrey, Cody Jordan, Paul Klinger, Ray Lagoe, Chip Leavitt, W. C. Longacre, Jimmy and Jo Lytle, Dan McCants, José Marmolejo, Chris Mathews, Dorothy Noble, Peter Ogura, Ken Patterson, Paul Paulson, the Penn Brothers, David Plotnikoff, Jim Raney, Glenn Rhodes, Richard Rice, Carol Shaugnessy, Robert Spiegel, Richard Sterling, Gina Stone, Jill Sullivan, John and Ann Swan, Lauren Swartzmiller, Arnold Talbott, Javier Vargas, Charlie Ward, Perfecta Wiggins, Mary Jane Wilan, F. P. Williamson, Gerry Wood, Phil Wood, and Henry Yamaoka.

INTRODUCTION

We cheerfully admit to being obsessed with peppers. Not only do we enjoy eating them, they have taken over the careers of us both!

During the past few years, we have noticed an enormous surge of interest in the subject of peppers, and much of the mail and phone calls received at the *Chile Pepper* magazine and New Mexico State University (NMSU) have concerned questions about pepper gardening. No book existed on the subject, but the information was available—scattered among hundreds of sources. We decided to track down the technical data, combine it with our own experiences of years of growing and breeding peppers, and create a single volume that would teach pepper gardening—and also be a reference for all pepper lovers.

For this book, we conducted what we call "The Great Pepper Grow-Out of 1992." In two plots, we cultivated nearly a thousand varieties of peppers to collect data and produce seed. In Las Cruces, the NMSU grow-out was part of a program to provide seed to the U.S. Department of Agriculture. In Albuquerque, we concentrated on home gardening techniques. There were greenhouses in both places for raising seedlings and growing peppers in containers.

We searched a vast amount of pepper literature for valuable growing information. We contacted hobbyists, researchers, and commercial growers all over the country to compile as much pepper gardening knowledge as possible.

Capsicum terminology can be confusing. Pepper, chili, chile, chilli, ají, paprika, and Capsicum are used interchangeably to describe the plants and pods of the genus *Capsicum*. Although "chile" is used

1

commonly in the Southwest and Latin America, we have chosen to use "pepper" in this book because it is the most common usage in the United States.

We have tried to avoid technical language where possible, and to explain the few specialized terms that we have used, but we request that the gardener take the time to learn about the genus and the five species of domesticated peppers. Doing so will make this book a lot easier to follow.

The pepper genus is *Capsicum*, from the Greek *kapto*, "to bite." It is pronounced CAP-see-coom. The species are:

annuum, meaning "annual," which is an incorrect designation; it is pronounced ANN-you-um and includes most of the common varieties, such as New Mexican, Jalapeño, Bell, and Wax

baccatum, meaning "berrylike"; it is pronounced both bah-COT-tum and bah-KAY-tum and consists of the South American peppers commonly known as *ajís*

chinense, meaning "from China," also an incorrect designation; it is pronounced chi-NEN-see and includes the extremely hot Habaneros

frutescens, meaning "shrubby" or "brushy"; it is pronounced fru-TES-enz and includes the familiar Tabascos

pubescens, meaning "hairy"; it is pronounced both pew-BES-enz and pu-BES-enz and includes the South American *rocotos*

In chapters 2 and 3, we describe the pod types and varieties of these species. Accepted botanical taxonomy has the genus and species name printed in italics and the varieties (subdivisions of the species) printed in italics if they are botanical (that is, wild) and in regular roman type and set off by single quotation marks if they are cultivated. The designation "cultivated variety" is commonly abbreviated to cultivar or cv. Thus we have:

Capsicum annuum cv. 'Jupiter', where the genus is *Capsicum*, the species is *annuum*, and the cultivated variety is 'Jupiter'

or

Capsicum frutescens var. *malagueta*, where the genus is *Capsicum*, the species is *frutescens*, and the variety is a botanical or wild variety, *malagueta*

Because the species, *annuum*, includes so many cultivars, an additional category has been added: a category that describes pod type. In this text, the names of the pod types have been set in regular roman type, but with no distinguishing quotation marks. Thus we have:

Capsicum annuum Bell 'Jupiter'

or

Capsicum chinense Habanero 'Rica Red'

Common names are set without capital letters if they are in English (for example, chile pepper), and in italics if they are in a foreign language (for example, *rocoto* is one of the common Spanish names for *Capsicum pubescens*).

Heat levels are expressed in Scoville Heat Units and are based on numerous tests using high-performance liquid chromatography. They are intended for comparison only, because heat levels can fluctuate greatly from pod to pod. Peppers range in heat from 0 to 300,000 Scoville Heat Units (the hottest pepper ever measured—a Habanero), although conceivably a pepper could measure as high as 1,000,000 Scoville Heat Units.

In growing the peppers, we prefer to use organic techniques whenever possible. In our home gardens, for example, we use only organic methods, and they produce satisfactory results. But on a commercial scale, when money is at stake, sometimes it is not feasible to grow peppers completely organically because the added costs are not recouped in the marketplace. If growers are, however, motivated by philosophical rather than economic reasons, by all means they should use organic methods. Gardeners should be warned that "organic" does not necessarily mean "safe." For example, organic certification usually allows nicotine sprays for the control of insects. Nicotine is an alkaloid and is highly to moderately toxic to humans, especially if inhaled.

We are very interested in the notes and observations of pepper gardeners for future additions to this book and for the increase and diffusion of pepper knowledge. Growers should feel free to send us material in care of The Chile Institute, Box 30003, Dept. 3Q, NMSU, Las Cruces, NM 88003.

CHAPTER 1

A Brief History of Pepper Growing

Peppers are finally getting credit for being among the most interesting and versatile plants grown. The pods are appealing for their brilliant colors, their interesting shapes, and their powerful pungency. The culinary uses of peppers have no limits, as is demonstrated by the proliferation of cookbooks about hot and spicy food. Extracts from the pods are used in food manufacturing, cosmetics, medicine, and even law enforcement. But despite their recent surge of popularity, confusion still exists about the history, nomenclature, and classification of the capsicums.

Classifying the *Capsicums*

Peppers are perennial subshrubs, native to South America, that are grown as annuals in colder climates. They are a part of the large nightshade family, or Solanaceae, and are closely related to tomato, potato, tobacco, and eggplant. They are not related to black pepper, *Piper nigrum*.

The genus *Capsicum* includes all the peppers, from the mild Bell to the hottest Habanero. There are twenty-seven species of *Capsicum* defined at this time, but confusion, argument, and change have haunted the nomenclature and classification of peppers from the beginning.

Robert Morrison, an English doctor-turned-botanist, described thirty-three species of peppers in his study, *Plantarum Historiae Universalis Oxoniensis*, published in 1680. In 1700, the Frenchman who gave the genus *Capsicum* its name, Joseph Pitton de Tournefort, de-

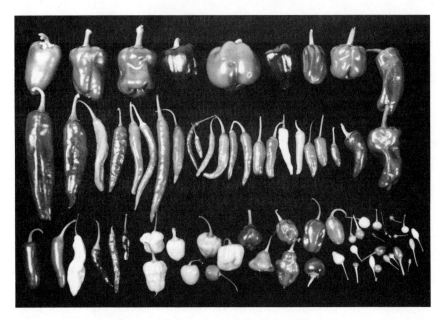

1.1 Variations in Pepper-Pod Shapes

termined that there were twenty-seven varieties of peppers in the genus. Fifty-three years later, Carolus Linnaeus, the famous Swedish botanist, classified peppers into just two species: *frutescens* (a perennial) and *annuum* (an annual).

By 1832, when K. A. Fingerhurth published his illustrated monograph on *Capsicums*, he divided the genus into twenty-five species. The number was up to fifty in 1852, when an amateur botanist, Felix Dunal, released his studies. As the botanist Charles Heiser observes, "More than eight species were [eventually] named, some of which were wild species but most were domesticated plants. To many botanists of the time, nearly every different type of fruit was thought to represent a distinct species."

In 1898, H. C. Irish, a botanist at the Missouri Botanical Gardens, returned to Linnaeus's original classification of two species and published *A Revision of the Genus Capsicum*. He, too, insisted that *frutescens* was a perennial species and *annuum* an annual one. Not so, countered L. H. Bailey, in his *Gentes Herbarum* (1923): The name *annuum* is a misnomer, because *annuums* can easily be grown as perennials in greenhouses and tropical regions. Bailey thus reduced *Capsicum* to a single species: *frutescens.*

Bailey launched a long-lasting trend toward classifying peppers as a single species. Others agreed but insisted calling that species *annuum*, not *frutescens*. Confusion reigned during the 1920s, 1930s, and 1940s as textbooks and periodicals used the two species names interchangeably. Finally, in 1948, the research of Paul G. Smith of the University of California and Charles B. Heiser of Indiana University proved that another *Capsicum* species did indeed exist: *pubescens*. The same team also determined the existence of *pendulum* (now called *baccatum*) in 1951. Also in that year, Smith and Heiser proved *frutescens* and *annuum* to be separate species, so now the count was up to four. In 1957, Smith and Heiser determined the independence of the *chinense* species, completing the current estimation of domesticated species at five.

Later work by the botanists W. Hardy Eshbaugh and Barbara Pickersgill determined that many of the undomesticated varieties of South American peppers were actually separate species, and a list published by Eshbaugh in 1983, based on the work of the Argentinian botanist Armando Hunziker, identified twenty-two undomesticated species. Wild peppers, like those described by Hunziker, still resemble their ancient ancestors.

The Origin and Spread of Peppers

Barbara Pickersgill, who is an ethnobotanist, believes that the first varieties of peppers originated in the remote geologic past in an area bordered by the mountains of southern Brazil to the east, by Bolivia to the west, and by Paraguay and northern Argentina to the south. This location is called a "nuclear area" and has the greatest concentration of wild species of peppers in the world. In this nuclear area, and only here, grow representatives of all the major domesticated species within the genus.

Over thousands of years, the peppers migrated from the nuclear area and eventually spread across the Americas. Scientists suspect that birds were primarily responsible for the spread of wild species from the nuclear area. The ancient wild peppers (like the wild varieties in all species today) had small, erect, red fruits that were very attractive to birds, which ate the pods whole. The extremely pungent pods did not bother the birds, and the seeds in those pods passed intact through

1.2   The Mother of All Peppers

the birds' digestive tracts and were deposited on the ground along with a perfect fertilizer. In this manner, peppers spread over the Western hemisphere long before the first Asian tribes crossed the Bering land bridge and settled the New World.

When humans first arrived in the Americas more than twelve thousand years ago, about twenty-five species of the genus *Capsicum* existed, of which five were later domesticated. Two of the five species, *baccatum* and *pubescens*, remained mostly in South America. *Baccatum*, known generically as *ají*, merely extended its range from southern Brazil west to the Pacific Ocean and became a domesticated pepper of choice in Bolivia, Ecuador, Peru, and Chile. Likewise, *Capsicum pubescens* migrated to the Andes, where it was domesticated, and later was called *rocoto* by the Spanish.

The three other domesticated species, *annuum*, *chinense*, and *frutescens* are closely related and shared a mutual, ancestral gene pool (meaning that genes were exchangeable among the species) known to botanists as the *annuum-chinense-frutescens* complex. These three species had spread far from the nuclear area and were in place when people arrived on the scene. Each species was domesticated independently—*annuum* in Mexico, *chinense* in Amazonia, and *frutes-*

cens in southern Central America. These three species have become the most commercially important peppers, and the story of their domestication and further spread is told in the archaeological record.

Taming the Wild Peppers

Peppers were probably in the human diet long before they were domesticated. The earliest evidence of peppers in contact with humans is from Mexico, where the archaeologist R. S. MacNeish discovered pepper seeds dating from about 7,500 B.C. during his excavations at Tamaulipas and Tehuacán. This find and an intact pod from Peru's Guitarrero Cave (dated 6,500 B.C.) seem to indicate that peppers were under cultivation approximately ten thousand years ago. That date is, however, extremely early for crop domestication and some experts suggest that these specimens are peppers that were harvested in the wild rather than cultivated by humans. The common bean (*Phaseolus vulgaris*) was also found in the same excavation levels, and scientists cannot be certain if they were wild or domesticated varieties. Experts are certain, however, that peppers were domesticated by at least 3,300 B.C.

Barbara Pickersgill theorizes that peppers were first accepted as "tolerated weeds." They were not cultivated but rather collected in the wild when the fruits were ripe. The wild forms had erect fruits that were deciduous, meaning that they separated easily from the calyx, and fell to the ground—another means, apart from birds, of spreading seeds. During the domestication process, early farmers, consciously or unconsciously, selected seeds from plants with larger, nondeciduous, and pendant fruits.

The larger fruits would provide a greater yield. Larger pods would become pendant and then would be hidden in the foliage and not stand above it as a beacon for pepper-hungry birds. The selection of varieties with the tendency to be nondeciduous ensured that the pods remained on the plant until fully ripe and thus were less likely to drop off as a result of wind or physical contact. The domesticated peppers gradually lost their natural means of seed dispersal by birds and became dependent upon human assistance. Because peppers cross-pollinate easily, hundreds—if not thousands—of varieties of peppers were developed. The five domesticated species have

9

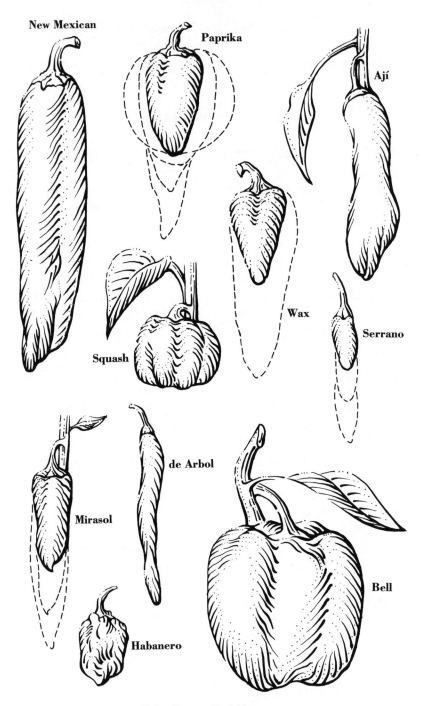

New Mexican

Paprika

Ají

Wax

Squash

Serrano

Mirasol

de Arbol

Bell

Habanero

1.3 Pepper Pod Shapes

10

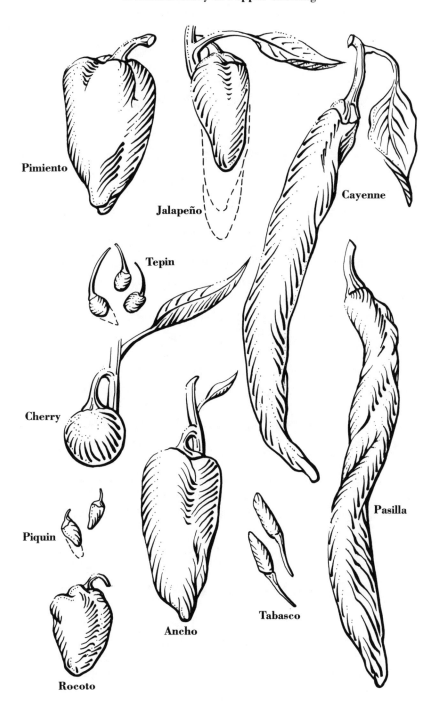

Pimiento

Jalapeño

Cayenne

Tepin

Cherry

Pasilla

Piquin

Ancho

Tabasco

Rocoto

hundreds of pod types (physically similar pods), and within each pod type are numerous varieties each with specific characteristics. These varieties are termed "cultivars" by horticulturists. In chapters 2 and 3 we describe the five species and their most commonly grown varieties in detail, but first a more general description is in order.

The Pepper Described

The pepper plant itself varies greatly in habit and size. Although some tropical pepper plants grow as high as 18 feet, the average height of the cultivated plants is less than 3 feet. The leaves of the *Capsicum* species vary between ¼ inch and 5 inches in length. They are usually ovate (egglike) in shape, arise singly, and develop alternately along the stem. The flowers are usually pendant, and their corolla colors are white or purple. Pollination occurs by wind in the case of self-pollination, or by insects, which can cause cross-pollination. Fruit-set is determined mostly by night temperatures, which should range between 55°F and 80°F.

The color, size, and shape of the pods varies enormously. Immature fruits may be green, yellow, white, or purple; ripe fruits may be red, orange, brown, yellow, green, or white. Their shapes may be round, conic, elongate, oblate, or bell-like. The pods range in size from ¼ inch to more than 17 inches long and are borne erect or pendant. Most varieties are ready to pick in the green stage after about 70 days and are fully ripened after about 130 days. Botanically speaking, the pods are berries, but horticulturists term them fruits. Harvested green, the pods are called a vegetable; harvested mature or dried, they become a spice.

Peppers in the United States

Peppers of the *annuum* species were transferred into what is now the American Southwest twice—first by birds and then by people. Botanists believe that the wild *annuum* variety known as *chiltepin* was spread northward from Mexico by birds long before Native Americans domesticated peppers and made them part of their trade goods.

These *chiltepins* still grow wild today in Arizona and in south Texas, where they are known as *chilipiquins*.

A debate rages over the second introduction of peppers into the Southwest. Most sources state that domesticated peppers were brought along with the settlement expedition of Juan de Oñate in 1598. Oñate crossed the Rio Grande near what is now El Paso and traveled north to what is now San Juan Pueblo near Santa Fe, where he founded the first Spanish town in the Southwest. But colonial documents that list the plants and animals brought along on the expedition do not mention peppers.

This lack of evidence has caused some researchers to conclude that peppers were transferred north in pre-Columbian times through trade between New Mexico's Pueblo Indians and the Toltecs of Central Mexico, which has been documented archaeologically. Squash and corn have been found in pre-Columbian digs in the Southwest; pepper seeds, however, have not been positively identified. Solanaceous seeds have been found, but their genus and species have not been determined.

So the date of the introduction of peppers into the United States is still unknown, but we do know that soon after the Spanish arrived, the cultivation of peppers in New Mexico spread rapidly and the pods were grown both in Spanish settlements and native pueblos. In fact, the cultivation was so dedicated that the peppers that were replanted in the same fields for centuries developed into land races that persist to this very day. These land races, such as 'Chimayó', 'Velarde', and 'Española', developed specific, indentifiable traits of pod shape, pungency, and maturation.

During the 1700s, peppers were popping up in other parts of the country. In 1768, according to legend, Minorcan settlers in St. Augustine, Florida, introduced the 'Datil' pepper, a land race of the *chinense* species. Supposedly, this pepper was transferred from the Caribbean to Africa and then to Minorca in the Mediterranean, from which it was brought to Florida. Some historians believe that this story is all bunk and that the 'Datil' peppers were introduced into Florida by trade with the Caribbean islands, a simpler explanation that makes a lot more sense. Other introductions were occurring during the eighteenth century as well. In 1785, George Washington planted two rows of what he called bird peppers and one row of Cayenne at Mount Vernon, but it is not known how he acquired the seed. Thomas Jefferson grew peppers from seed imported from Mexico.

By the early 1800s, commercial seed varieties became available to the American public. In 1806, a botanist named McMahon listed four varieties for sale, and in 1826, another botanist named Thornburn listed 'Long' (Cayenne), 'Tomato-Shaped' (Squash), 'Bell' (Oxheart), 'Cherry', and 'Bird' (West Indian) peppers as being available for gardeners. Two years later, Squash peppers were being cultivated in North American gardens and that same year (1828), the 'California Wonder Bell' pepper was first named and grown commercially. (A hundred years later, in 1928, this same pepper was released as an official variety, known as the 'Calwonder Bell'.)

At around this same time, travelers and historians were beginning to notice the influence of chile peppers in the rather primitive American Southwest. "The extravagant use of red pepper among the [New] Mexicans has become truly proverbial. It enters into nearly every dish at every meal, and often so predominates as entirely to conceal the character of the viands," wrote Josiah Gregg in 1844 in his book *The Commerce of the Prairies*.

In 1849, the first mention of Tabasco peppers occurred in the *New Orleans Daily Delta* of 7 December: "I must not omit to notice the Colonel's pepper patch, which is two acres in extent, all planted with a new species of red pepper, which Colonel White has introduced into our country, called Tobasco red pepper." The colonel referred to is Maunsel White, one of the earliest growers of Tabasco peppers.

These *frutescens* peppers, introduced into Louisiana from Tabasco, Mexico, were soon grown in quantity by Edmund McIlhenny of Avery Island, who transformed them from obscurity into one of the most famous peppers in history. Experimenting with Tabasco peppers, which he mashed, salted, aged, and then strained and mixed with vinegar, McIlhenny soon produced his famous Tabasco sauce. In 1868, the first 350 bottles of sauce were shipped to wholesalers, and by 1870 McIlhenny obtained a patent for Tabasco brand hot-pepper sauce. The rest is history, as Tabasco became the best-known and best-selling hot sauce in the world. Two excellent books in which the history, growing, and processing of Tabasco peppers are discussed are *Hot Peppers* by Richard Schweid (Ten Speed Press, 1989) and *Peppers: A Story of Hot Pursuits* by Amal Naj (Knopf, 1992).

During the time that Tabascos were being grown in Louisiana, the introduction of European varieties of peppers into the United States began. In 1867, the 'Sweet Spanish' variety arrived from France; initially it was called 'Crimson Queen'. By 1888, the Burpee Seed Company offered twenty varieties of peppers, including 'Celestial', 'Red Squash' ("of Massachusetts origin"), the 'Spanish Monstrous' (6 to 8 inches long), 'Red Chili' ("best for pepper sauce"), the 'Long Yellow', and the 'Cranberry', said to look like one. Burpee's Farm Annual was the first in a long line of seed catalogs offering many varieties of peppers, most of which were discontinued or transformed. The number of varieties available—and their nomenclature—is a problem that will continue to vex botanists, horticulturists, farmers, and home gardeners.

Meanwhile, things were heating up in the West. In 1896, Emilio Ortega, at one time the sheriff of Ventura County, California, brought back pepper seeds with him after a visit to New Mexico. He planted them near Anaheim, and they adapted well to the soil and climate there. By the time Ortega opened the first pepper-canning operation in Ventura in 1898, the pod type that originated in New Mexico was known as Anaheim, a name that would stick long after Anaheim was paved over and turned into Disneyland. (In 1987, the name of the pod type was changed to the more accurate New Mexican, and 'Anaheim' became a variety of the New Mexican pod type.)

Around the turn of the century, botanists were having a field day cataloging the bewildering number of varieties of peppers. In 1898, H. C. Irish named forty-three different varieties, and by 1902 W. W. Tracy of the U.S. Department of Agriculture, listing 114 pepper varieties in the United States, of which half were Bells, noted: "There is such an indiscriminate use of epithets as to make the distinctions of varieties very bewildering. . . . One great source of the confusion in variety names . . . is the use of descriptive words and phrases in multiplying names which frequently mark no varietal differences." An example Tracy used was 'Ruby King', which had such incarnations as 'Mammoth Ruby King', 'Maule's Ruby King', and 'Burpee Ruby King'. Some now-common pod types, such as Squash, Bell, Cayenne, and Cherry, also appeared on his list.

In 1907, Fabian Garcia, a horticulturist at the Agricultural Experiment Station at the College of Agriculture and Mechanical Arts in Las Cruces, New Mexico (now New Mexico State University),

1.4   Fabian Garcia

began his first experiments in breeding more standardized pepper varieties and, in 1908, published "Chile Culture," the first bulletin on peppers from the Agricultural Experiment Station.

By 1910, the Agricultural Census listed 1,641 farms in the United States growing peppers on a total of 3,483 acres, the average being 3.2 acres. The top four states in pepper production were New Jersey, California, Florida, and New Mexico (which was still a territory at the time).

More European varieties were being introduced. In 1911, the first Pimientos from Spain arrived in Georgia. In Spalding County, S. D. Riegel, a talented farmer, developed a line of Pimientos from Spain that eventually was released as 'Perfection Pimiento' in 1913. In 1915 and 1916, the South also witnessed the first American production of Paprika—in South Carolina. Ninety-one tons were produced but the crop was soon abandoned in favor of cotton.

Meanwhile, back in New Mexico, Fabian Garcia, who became director of the Experiment Station in 1913, expanded his breeding program. In 1917, after ten years of experiments with various strains of Pasilla chiles, Garcia released 'New Mexico No. 9', the first attempt to produce a variety of chile with a dependable pod size and heat level. The variety became the standard chile in New Mexico until 1950.

By 1919, the total U.S. acreage in peppers was 15,290, valued at $3.1 million. Seven years later, the acreage in seven important states was about the same (15,430), but the value had climbed to $5 million. New Jersey led all states with 7,500 acres. Between 1930 and 1950, chile pepper acreage in New Mexico averaged between 900 and 1,200 acres.

Duplicate varieties of peppers, about which W. W. Tracy had complained in 1902, were gradually phased out of seed catalogs, and by 1930 American seed producers recorded that a mere thirty different varieties were available. That year, the botanist H. C. Irish, writing in *The Standard Cyclopedia of Horticulture*, noted: "Peppers are classed as one of the minor vegetables in that they have not been grown in large quantities in any one locality and the aggregate production is smaller than the so-called truck crops, such as tomatoes, cucumbers, and the like. During the last decade there has been a decided increase in acreage."

There was a flurry of activity during the 1930s as acreage increased but value dropped because of the Great Depression. In 1931, Paprika production began in southern California, and the following year Hungarian Wax peppers were introduced into the United States from Hungary. In that same year, A. T. Erwin, a botanist at Iowa State University, bucked the trend of declining numbers of varieties and named 153 different varieties of peppers!

In 1935, H. L. Cochran of the Georgia Experiment Station estimated that 17,000 acres of "green peppers" (undoubtedly Bells) were under cultivation, worth a paltry $2.2 million. The thirties also marked the development of the 'Truhart Perfection Pimiento' in Georgia, and by 1935 Georgia had 11,000 acres of Pimientos under cultivation, valued at $450,000.

From 1940 to 1957, sweet pepper acreage in the United States doubled to more than 44,000 acres, and in 1941 the first Hungarian Paprika seeds were planted in Washington's Yakima Valley. By 1949, Paprika production had been resumed in South Carolina and Louisiana by immigrants from Yugoslavia, but the industry was not successful. The year 1950 marked the introduction of 'New Mexico

No. 6' by Roy Harper of New Mexico State University, and that variety became the standard grown in New Mexico. That same year, the Georgia Pimiento crop was 32,000 acres, valued at $3.15 million. Meanwhile, California produced 3,850 tons of dry red chile, valued at $3 million, on 3,932 acres—a yield that would eventually increase.

The Bell pepper crop exploded after World War II, and by 1951 production rose to 105,000 tons worth $16.8 million on 34,700 acres. Chile pepper acreage had increased to about 8,500 acres by 1954. The 1950s also witnessed the introduction of many new varieties, including 'Fresno' (in 1952 by the Clarence Brown Seed Co.), 'Carolina Hot' (a variety of Cayenne, in 1954), 'Sandía' (a variety of New Mexican by Roy Harper in 1956), 'New Mexico No. 6-4' (in 1957, which became, and still is, the number-one variety of chile pepper grown in the United States), and 'Cubanelle' (in 1958, from Italy).

During the 1960s, the popularity of chili con carne cook-offs increased the awareness of chile peppers, especially in Texas and California. The Chili Appreciation Society—International (CASI), which had been founded in 1951, had more than two hundred "Pods" (chapters) in Texas during the mid-fifties, and a similar organization, the International Chili Society (ICS) was formed in California. Other notable events in the 1960s: Roy Nakayama took over the chile pepper breeding program at New Mexico State University from Roy Harper in 1960, and California Paprika production reached 2,900 tons in 1963.

By the 1970s peppers were reaching a wider audience. In 1970, Ben Villalon founded the Texas pepper breeding program at the Agricultural Experiment Station in Weslaco. That same year, Dr. Walter Greenleaf of Auburn University bred 'Greenleaf Tabasco', a variety resistant to tobacco mosaic virus. In 1973, the first meeting of the National Pepper Conference was held, proof that peppers were finally being regarded as a serious crop plant in this country. During 1975, chile pepper acreage in New Mexico climbed to 9,200 and Roy Nakayama released 'NuMex Big Jim', a variety that produces the longest pods of any chile pepper—pods up to an astounding seventeen inches have been reported. The first cookbook solely devoted to hot and spicy foods, *The Hellfire Cookbook* by John Cranwell, was published in 1975. During the next twenty-seven years, twenty-three similar titles would follow as cooks in the United States discovered chile peppers and hot and spicy foods. But sweet peppers were gaining ground, too, and by the end of the decade Bell pepper acreage topped 100,000 for the first time.

In 1980, Tom Williams, a vegetable breeder at Rogers NK seed company, introduced the 'Jupiter' variety of Bell pepper, which soon became the leading pepper variety cultivated in the country. The following year, Ben Villalon at Weslaco introduced 'TAM Mild Jalapeño-1', which was only one-third as hot as the standard Jalapeño. It became an immediate hit with growers and consumers, who usually ate them with nachos. Also during the early 1980s, chile pepper acreage in New Mexico topped 17,000, with an additional 5,594 in California and 1,980 in Texas. Louisiana hot pepper acreage was about 200.

In 1983, the 'Española Improved' variety was released after years of testing by Frank B. Matta at the Española Valley Branch Experiment Station in Alcalde, New Mexico. The variety was developed for cool climates to produce substantial quantities of both green and red pods. The following year, Jean Andrews published her landmark study, *Peppers: The Domesticated Capsicums*, which was the first attempt in book form to organize, describe, and illustrate the major pod types of the five domesticated species. Sales of the book proved that there was a great interest in all aspects of pepper lore.

Despite Dr. Andrews's accomplishment, botanists were *still* debating the number of pepper varieties. In 1985, Charles Heiser's answer to the question was: "There can be no definite answer to that question . . . except to say that there are lots of different kinds of peppers." Later, in 1987, the horticulturist Paul G. Smith would add: "The tremendous variation in fruit size, shape, and color, as well as an extremely variable plant habit in *C. annuum* alone make it impossible to devise a practical system of classification that would cover the large numbers of forms known to be cultivated."

Undaunted, coauthor Paul W. Bosland, who took over the chile pepper breeding program at New Mexico State University in 1986, devised the "species, pod type, variety" system of identification (i.e., *Capsicum annuum*, New Mexican, 'NuMex Big Jim'), in *Capsicum Pepper Varieties and Classification* (1989), the method most commonly used today. Other significant events in the world of peppers in the 1980s were the founding of *The Whole Chile Pepper* magazine (later, just *Chile Pepper*) by Robert Spiegel in 1987, the first conference on the wild *chiltepin*, hosted in 1988 by Gary Nabhan at the Desert Botanical Gardens in Phoenix, and the beginning of Habanero production in California and Texas in 1989. By the end of the decade, chile pepper acreage in New Mexico had climbed to 23,650 and nationwide it topped 30,000 for the first time.

By the 1990s chile peppers had come into their own. *The Whole Chile Pepper Book* by Dave DeWitt and Nancy Gerlach (Little, Brown, 1990) soon had more than fifty thousand copies in print. In 1991, Mark Miller wrote *The Great Chile Book* (Ten Speed Press), an illustrated guide to fresh and dry pepper varieties, most originating in Mexico. That same year, acreage of Tabascos under cultivation in Louisiana dropped to a low of 75, and the plants were used mostly for seed.

Also in 1991, Bell pepper distribution in the United States reached 219,300 tons (including imports), up from the year before by 23,550 tons. The top Bell-producing states were Florida, California, New Jersey, Texas, North Carolina, and Georgia. Top importing countries were Mexico and the Netherlands. Also in 1991, The Chile Institute was founded at New Mexico State University to assemble a permanent archive of information about *Capsicums*. It is a nonprofit organization that publishes bibliographies and a newsletter to promote chile peppers worldwide.

In 1993, as this book goes to press, pepper growing has reached an all-time high in this country. Harvested acres of chile peppers are expected to top 36,000 in New Mexico, an increase of more than 400 percent since 1975. Imported peppers are up, too, with the "Balance of Chiles Deficit" topping $36 million (see below). There seems to be no end in sight to the love of peppers in the United States.

The Balance of Chiles Deficit

In 1991, the United States exported 2.6 metric tons of capsicums worth $6.5 million, up nearly $1.5 million from the previous year. Most of them went to Canada, Mexico, and Germany. But, because total imports of capsicums were $42.6 million, the Balance of Chiles Deficit for 1991 came to $36.1 million—triple the 1988 deficit.

Statistics released by the U.S. Departments of Commerce and Agriculture in April 1992 revealed that in 1991 imports of Ancho and New Mexican chiles actually declined from the previous year, though the dollar value was higher. The vast majority of imported Anchos and New Mexican chiles, nearly fourteen hundred metric tons, came from Mexico, with only minor quantities being imported from Hong Kong, Chile, and Israel. However, imports of other capsicums came from twenty-five countries, with a total value of $24.8 million, up nearly $5 million from the previous year. Leading the way were Mexico, Chile, China, India, Pakistan, and Turkey. For statistics on worldwide pepper production, see the Appendix.

The fact that the Balance of Chiles Deficit nearly tripled in three years reveals that hot pepper growers in the United States are not keeping up with domestic demand. We believe that opportunities abound for both small- and large-scale pepper growers in this country. Maybe in some small way this book can help turn the deficit around by convincing people to grow more peppers!

CHAPTER 2

Pod Types and Varieties of *Capsicum annuum*

The most likely ancestor of the common *annuum* varieties grown in the garden today is the wild *chiltepin* (*Capsicum annuum* var. *aviculare*). It has a wide distribution, from South America to southern Arizona, but the cultivated *annuums* were originally concentrated in Mexico and Central America. This situation suggests that *annuums* were domesticated in Mexico, possibly as early as 7,500 B.C., but more likely around 2,500 B.C.

By the time the Spanish arrived in Mexico, Aztec plant breeders had already developed dozens of *annuum* varieties. According to Bernardino de Sahagún, a historian who lived in Mexico in 1529, "hot green peppers, smoked peppers, water peppers, tree peppers, beetle peppers, and sharp-pointed red peppers" existed. Undoubtedly, these peppers were the precursors to the large number of *annuum* varieties found in Mexico today. Christopher Columbus took *annuum* seeds back to the Old World, and they were planted extensively in the Portuguese and Spanish colonies, resulting in even more diversification of the species.

C. annuum is the most extensively cultivated species in the world, both commercially and in home gardens. It is the principal species grown in Hungary, India, Mexico, China, Korea, and the East Indies. Because the peppers cross-pollinate so easily, probably thousands of different varieties exist around the world. Each has a common name, making identification difficult. In Mexico, for example, more than two hundred common names for peppers are used—but only about fifteen *annuum* pod types are cultivated commercially.

Annuums used to be divided into two categories: sweet (or mild) peppers and hot (or chile) peppers. Modern plant breeding has, however, removed that distinction. Now hot Bell varieties and sweet Jalapeño and New Mexican varieties have been bred.

Gardeners should remember that hundreds of varieties exist; we have selected for this book those that we think are most representative and most available. The full names and addresses of the seed sources are given in the Resources.

Ancho/Poblano

The name Ancho means "wide," an allusion to the broad, flat, heart-shaped pods of the dried form. The fresh pod is called *poblano*.

The Plant

Anchos are multiple-stemmed and compact to semierect, semiwoody, and about 25 inches high. The dark green and shiny leaves are approximately 4 inches long and 2½ inches wide.

Flowers and Pods

The corollas are white and appear at every node. The flowering period begins fifty days after sowing and continues until the first frost. The pods are pendant, vary between 3 and 6 inches long, and are from 2 to 3 inches wide. They are conical or truncated and have indented shoulders. Immature pods are dark green, maturing to either red or brown. The dried pods are a very dark reddish brown, nearly black. They are fairly mild, ranging from 1,000 to 1,500 Scoville Heat Units.

Cultivation

The Ancho/Poblano varieties grow well in the United States. Bill Irvine, quoted in *Organic Gardening*, reported that his plants grown in Wharton, New Jersey, topped four feet and he needed to stake them to keep them from toppling over. They produced well, but the pods did not mature to the red stage before the end of the growing season. The usual growing period is between 100 and 120

2.1   Ancho/Poblano

days and the yield is about fifteen pods per plant, although Irvine reported obtaining up to thirty pods per plant.

Uses

Fresh Poblanos may be roasted and peeled, then preserved by canning or freezing. They are often stuffed to make *chiles rellenos*. The dried pods can be stored in airtight containers for months, or they can be ground into a powder. Anchos are commonly used in sauces called *moles*.

Recommended Varieties

'Ancho' or 'Poblano' (generic).
   SEED SOURCES: Alfrey, Enchanted Seeds, Hudson, Nichols, Old Southwest, Park, Redwood City Seed, Seeds of Change, Seeds West, Shepherd's

'Ancho 101'. Black-green pods turning brown-red.
   SEED SOURCES: Porter, Rocky Mountain, Tomato Grower's, Westwind

'Mulato'. Ripe pod turns brown.
   SEED SOURCE: Enchanted Seeds

'Negro'. Mild pods turn black when dried.

SEED SOURCES: Native Seeds, Redwood City Seed

Bell

Commercially, Bells are the most commonly grown peppers in the United States. More than a hundred varieties of Bell peppers have been bred, and we have made our selections on the basis of color, pungency, disease resistance, and availability to the home grower.

The Plant

The Bells are multistemmed with a habit that is subcompact tending toward prostrate, growing 1 to 2½ feet tall. The leaves are medium green, ovate to lanceolate, smooth, and are about 3 inches long and 1½ inches wide.

Flowers and Pods

The flower corollas are white with no spots. The pods are pendant, three- or four-lobed, blocky, and blunt. Their immature color is dark green, usually maturing to red, but sometimes to yellow, orange, or brown. The pungent varieties have only a slight bite, ranging from 100 to 600 Scoville Heat Units.

Cultivation

Bells grow well in sandy loams with good drainage. The hotter varieties are usually grown in the home garden. The growing period ranges from eighty to one hundred days, depending on whether the peppers are picked green or at the mature color. A single plant produces between ten and twenty pods.

Use

Most Bells are used fresh, cut up in salads or stuffed and baked. Pungent Bells are also used in fresh salsas. Both kinds can be preserved by freezing.

Recommended Varieties

'Ace'. Very early maturing (fifty-five days), for cold climates.
SEED SOURCES: Gurney, High Altitude

'Ariane'. Dutch hybrid, deep orange pods, disease resistant.
SEED SOURCE: Shepherd's

'Big Bertha'. Huge pods, 7 to 8 inches long and 4 inches wide, weight to 1 pound, no heat.
SEED SOURCES: Gurney, Field's, Liberty

'California Wonder'. Large, mild pods.
SEED SOURCES: Gurney, Field's, Harris, Liberty, Nichols, Pinetree, Porter, Territorial Seed, Twilley

'Chocolate'. Brown pods turning red, no heat.
SEED SOURCES: High Altitude, Johnny's, Seeds of Change

'Corona'. Orange pods at maturity, no heat.
SEED SOURCE: Johnny's

'French Red Bell'. A hybrid from France, maturing red.
SEED SOURCE: Seeds West

'Gypsy'. Yellow pods, very early maturing, no heat.
SEED SOURCES: Burpee, Gurney, Field's, Harris, Hastings, High Altitude, Liberty, Nichols, Rocky Mountain

2.2 Bell

'Ivory'. Hybrid, turns from creamy white to pale yellow to orange.
   SEED SOURCE: Shepherd's

'Karlo'. Yellow pods turning red, mildly hot.
   SEED SOURCE: Seeds of Change

'Lilac'. Hybrid, changing from lavender to lilac to deep red.
   SEED SOURCE: Shepherd's

'Mexi-Bell'. A hybrid, mildly hot pepper (500 Scoville Heat Units or less) with the Bell taste.
   SEED SOURCES: Burpee, Enchanted Seeds, Park, Plants/Southwest, Porter, Rocky Mountain, Tomato Grower's, Twilley

'Orobelle'. Hybrid, with deep yellow pods.
   SEED SOURCE: Tomato Grower's

'Purple Beauty'. Immature pods are purple.
   SEED SOURCES: Gurney, Field's, Harris, Hastings, Hudson, Liberty, Nichols, Park, Pinetree, Porter, Seeds of Change, Tomato Grower's

Cayenne

No one seems to know the origin of this type. Although it was named after the Cayenne River in French Guiana, it is not grown in South America. Some speculate that the Portuguese may have transferred it to Europe, then to Africa and India, where it appears today in many forms.

The Plant

The Cayenne is treelike, with multiple stems and an erect habit. It grows up to 3 feet tall and 2 feet wide. The leaves are ovate, smooth, and medium green, about 3½ inches wide and 2 inches long.

Flowers and Pods

The flower corollas are white with no spots. The pods are pendant, long, and slender, measuring up to 10 inches long and 1 inch wide. They are often wrinkled and irregular in shape. A mature plant can easily produce forty pods. The Cayenne is very pungent, measuring between 30,000 and 50,000 Scoville Heat Units.

Cultivation

The Cayenne has a growing period of about ninety days. Surprisingly, perhaps, most of the Cayennes used in the hot sauces made in Louisiana are grown in New Mexico.

Use

Although the immature green Cayennes can be used fresh in salsas, the most common use is to grind the dried red pods into powder. They are also crushed into flakes (such as the sort found in pizza parlors). In Louisiana, numerous hot sauces are made with Cayennes.

Recommended Varieties

'Cayenne' (generic).
SEED SOURCES: Enchanted Seeds, Nichols, Pinetree, Plants/Southwest, Rocky Mountain, Seeds of Change, Westwind

'Hot Portugal'. Large, 8-inch, medium-hot pods.
SEED SOURCE: Seeds of Change

'Large Thick'. Wrinkled, 6-inch, very hot pods.
SEED SOURCES: Liberty, Old Southwest, Tomato Grower's, Twilley

2.3   Cayenne

'Long Slim'. Hot, 6-inch pods.
  SEED SOURCES: Burpee, Enchanted Seeds, Field's, Hastings, Liberty, Park, Porter, Redwood City Seed, Rocky Mountain, Territorial Seed, Tomato Grower's

'Ring of Fire'. Hot, 4-inch pods.
  SEED SOURCE: Seeds of Change

'Super Cayenne'. Hybrid, with 3½-inch hot pods.
  SEED SOURCES: Burpee, Park, Tomato Grower's, Twilley

Cherry

The resemblance of the pods to giant cherries is the reason this type is called Cherry. This pepper is familiar because the pods are commonly pickled and served as an accompaniment to sandwiches.

The Plant

The Cherry has single stems and an erect habit, and grows about 2 feet tall. The leaves are smooth, dark green, and about 3 inches long and 1½ inches wide.

Flowers and Pods

The flower corollas are white with no spots. The pods are erect and spherical, measuring about 1¾ inches wide. At maturity, they are orange or red and are fairly mild to moderately pungent, measuring from 0 to about 3,500 Scoville Heat Units.

Cultivation

Some gardeners grow the Cherry type as an ornamental, and it does well in the home garden.

Use

The pods can be used fresh in salads, but are most commonly pickled.

2.4   Cherry

Recommended Varieties

'Cherry Sweet'. One-inch pods good for pickling, no heat.
SEED SOURCES: Burpee, Enchanted Seeds, Hastings, Nichols,
Porter, Rocky Mountain, Territorial Seed, Twilley

'Cherrytime'. Mildly hot, 2-inch pods, ripening red.
SEED SOURCE: Johnny's

'Red Cherry Hot'. Round, 1½-inch, medium-hot pods.
SEED SOURCES: Enchanted Seeds, Harris, Hastings, Liberty,
Nichols, Porter, Twilley

Cuban

These mild pods are much loved when fried. There are two basic
types: the long-fruited ones, such as 'Key Largo' and 'Biscayne', and
the short-fruited types, such as 'Cubanelle'.

The Plant

Cuban varieties are upright, medium tall, between 26 and 36
inches high, and yield heavily. The leaves are light green, not as dense
as those of Bells, and are 3 inches long and 1½ inches wide.

31

Flowers and Pods

The flower corollas are white with no spots. The pods are pendant, long, and slender, measuring between 2 and 10 inches long and up to 2 inches wide. Some taper to a thin point. The immature pods are yellowish green, maturing to red. Most Cuban varieties are not pungent, although some may measure up to 500 Scoville Heat Units.

Cultivation

The cultivation is identical to that of Bells. The yield is twelve fruits per plant or more.

Use

The thin flesh of this type is very flavorful, so it has become a substitute for Bells. The pods are used in salads, are pickled, and in Florida are usually fried.

2.5 Cuban

Recommended Varieties

'Aconagua'. Huge, 11-inch, pale green pods with no heat.
    SEED SOURCE: Tomato Grower's

'Biscayne'. Hybrid, with pale green, 6-inch pods with no heat.
    SEED SOURCES: Park, Porter, Tomato Grower's, Twilley

'Cubanelle'. Yellow, 6-inch pods with no heat.
    SEED SOURCES: Enchanted Seeds, Harris, Hudson, Liberty, Park,
    Pinetree, Porter, Rocky Mountain, Territorial Seed, Tomato
    Grower's, Twilley

'Key Largo'. Large, 7-inch, yellow-green pods turning orange-red;
    a hybrid.
    SEED SOURCE: Harris

'Montego'. Seven- to 9-inch pods, pale yellow-white, no heat.
    SEED SOURCE: Johnny's

'Pepperoncini'. Small, 3- to 4-inch, mild pods.
    SEED SOURCES: Nichols, Porter, Shepherd's, Tomato Grower's

De Arbol

The name of this Mexican type means "treelike," an allusion to the
appearance of the mature plant. Some sources list de Arbol with Cayenne, a false grouping.

The Plant

The de Arbol type has multiple stems and an erect habit. It
grows up to 3 feet tall, often resembling a small tree. The leaves vary
from smooth to hairy, are light green in color, and are small—about
1¼ inches long and about ½ inch wide.

Flowers and Pods

The flower corollas are white with no spots. The pods are pendant, occasionally erect, elongate, and are about 3 inches long and ⅜
inch wide. They are green, often maturing to red; yellow and orange

2.6   De Arbol

varieties have been developed. The pods are hot, measuring between 15,000 and 30,000 Scoville Heat Units.

Cultivation

It does well in the home garden and has a growing period of about eighty days.

Use

The pods are often either ground into a powder to be added to cooked sauces, or combined with water and vinegar to make table sauces. De Arbols are also used to make wreaths and *ristras*.

Recommended Varieties

'De Arbol' (generic). Long, thin, hot, red pods.
SEED SOURCES: Native Seeds, Old Southwest, Redwood City Seed, Seeds of Change

'NuMex Sunburst'. Bright orange, 3-inch, medium-hot pods.
SEED SOURCE: Enchanted Seeds

'NuMex Sunflare'. Bright red, 3-inch, medium-hot pods.
SEED SOURCE: Enchanted Seeds

'NuMex Sunglo'. Bright yellow, 3-inch, medium-hot pods.
SEED SOURCE: Enchanted Seeds

Exotics

The catch-all name "Exotics" refers to land races of hot peppers grown primarily in the Eastern hemisphere that have been imported into the United States for home gardens. The pods usually resemble those of Cayennes or Piquins.

The Plant

There is enormous variation in plant habit. The favorite varieties, such as 'Thai Hot', have multiple stems, an erect habit, and are about 18 inches high. The leaves are small, medium green in color, and are about 2 inches long and ½ inch wide.

Flowers and Pods

The flower corollas are white with no spots. The pods are usually borne erect, several at each node. They are elongate and pointed, measuring about 2½ inches long and ½ to ¾ inch wide. Most of the Exotics are quite hot, measuring between 30,000 and 100,000 Scoville Heat Units.

Cultivation

The growing period is between eighty and ninety days, and the Exotics do well in home gardens. Gerry Wood, a pepper hobbyist in Nashville, Tennessee, grows an Exotic variety called 'Pili-Pili', which he "imported" into the United States after a trip to Togo in West Africa. The Cayenne-like plants grow to about 3 feet tall and are loaded with extremely hot, 2-inch pods. Pat Kiewicz grows 'Thai Hots' in Michigan and reports that they produce very well. Lauren Swartsmiller has "prolific harvests" from her 'Thai Hots' grown in containers of various sizes in southeastern New York.

Use

The dried pods are used in stir-fry dishes or ground into powder.

Recommended Varieties

'Berbere'. Extremely hot, 6-inch pods from Ethiopia.
SEED SOURCE: Seeds of Change

'Calistan'. Long, thin, hot pods from Turkey.
SEED SOURCE: Redwood City Seed

'Pili-Pili'. Long, thin, hot pods from Africa.
SEED SOURCE: Pepper Gal

'Thai Hot'. Erect, 1-inch, very hot pods.
SEED SOURCES: Enchanted Seeds, Park, Sunrise

'Yatsafusa'. Very hot, 3-inch pods from Japan.
SEED SOURCE: Nichols

2.7   Pod Variations in the 'Thai' Varieties

36

Jalapeño

Named after the city of Xalapa in Mexico (where it is no longer grown), the Jalapeño is probably the most famous chile pepper. It is often the pepper of choice for pepper-eating contests.

The Plant

Jalapeños usually grow between 2½ and 3 feet tall. Fred Melton of Jacksonville, Florida, has grown one that reached 12 feet, 3 inches. Jalapeños may have a compact single stem or an upright, multi-branched, spreading habit. The leaves are light to dark green and measure about 3 inches long and 2 inches wide.

Flowers and Pods

The flower corollas are white with no spots. The pods, which are conical and cylindrical, are pendant and about 3 inches long and 1 inch wide. They are green (occasionally sunlight will cause purpling), mature to red, and measure between 2,500 and 10,000 Scoville Heat Units. The fruits may have a thin, edible netting around them, which is called "corkiness." This trait is considered desirable in Mexico, but not in the United States (although it is becoming more accepted).

Cultivation

U.S. varieties are adapted to semiarid climates; Mexican varieties do better in hot and humid areas. The growing period is between seventy and eighty days, and the yield is between about twenty-five and thirty-five pods per plant.

Use

Most Jalapeños from the home garden are used fresh in salsas, sliced into rings for nachos, or pickled. Smoke-dried Jalapeños, known as *chipotles*, are sold in their dried form or canned in an *adobo* sauce.

2.8   Jalapeño

Recommended Varieties

'Early Jalapeño'. Very hot, fruits early.
SEED SOURCES: Seed sources: Harris, Johnny's, Rocky Mountain, Shepherd's, Territorial Seed

'Jalapa'. Hybrid.
SEED SOURCES: Porter, Rocky Mountain, Twilley

'Jalapeño' (generic).
SEED SOURCES: Field's, Gurney, Old Southwest, Porter, Rocky Mountain, Sunrise, Seeds West

'Jalapeño M'. Large, dark green, mild pods.
SEED SOURCES: Burpee, Harris, Liberty, Plants/Southwest, Twilley

'Mitla'. Large, hot, early pods.
SEED SOURCES: Porter, Twilley

'TAM Jalapeño'. Mildly pungent flavor.
SEED SOURCES: Enchanted Seeds, Gurney, Nichols, Park, Porter, Rocky Mountain, Territorial Seed, Twilley

Mirasol

The name means "looking at the sun" in Spanish, an allusion to the erect pods of some varieties.

The Plant

Mirasols have an intermediate number of stems, an erect habit tending toward compact, and grow between 2 and 3 feet high. The leaves are smooth and medium green, 2 inches long and 1¼ inches wide.

Flowers and Pods

The flower corollas are white with no spots. The fruits are borne either erect or pendant, are usually elongate and pointed, and measure 4 inches long and ¾ inch wide. The pods of some varieties, such as 'Cascabel', are round. The mature pods are dark red. Mirasol varieties measure between 2,500 and 5,000 Scoville Heat Units.

2.9   Mirasol

Cultivation

Mirasols are very popular in Mexico but uncommon in home gardens in the United States. The growing period is at least ninety days, and the yield is about fifty pods per plant.

Use

The pods are usually dried and can be ground into powder. They are used in sauces, soups, stews, and meat dishes.

Recommended Varieties

'Mirasol' (generic). Hot.
  SEED SOURCES: Enchanted Seeds, Native Seeds

'De Comida'. A Guajillo with 5-inch pods, medium hot.
  SEED SOURCE: Hudson

'Guajillo', or 'Costeño'. Thin-walled, 3- to 4-inch pods, hot.
  SEED SOURCES: Redwood City Seed, Seeds of Change

'Mexican Improved'. Very hot with yellow-red pods.
  SEED SOURCE: Plants/Southwest

'NuMex Mirasol'. Clusters of 3- to 4-inch pods.
  SEED SOURCE: Enchanted Seeds

New Mexican

This type, with long green pods that turn red, is the chile pepper of choice for Mexican-style cooked sauces in the United States. It has been cultivated in New Mexico for more than three hundred years. Formerly, the pod type was called Anaheim, but now the 'Anaheim' is considered a variety of the New Mexican pod type.

The Plant

The plant has mostly a compact habit with an intermediate number of stems, and grows between 20 and 30 inches high. The leaves

2.10   New Mexican

are ovate, medium green, fairly smooth, and about 3 inches long and 2 inches wide.

Flowers and Pods

The flower corollas are white with no spots. The pods are pendant, elongate, bluntly pointed, and measure between 4 and 12 inches long. They are dark green, maturing to various shades of red. Their heat ranges from quite mild to medium, between 500 and 2,500 Scoville Heat Units.

Cultivation

The growing period is about eighty days, and each plant produces between ten and twenty pods, depending on variety and cultural techniques.

Use

New Mexican chiles are used in either their green or red forms. Green chiles may be roasted and peeled, then used fresh for stuffed chiles or sauces, or canned, frozen, or dried (*chile pasado*). Red chiles are usually kept on the bush until they become leathery. Then they are tied into strings, or *ristras*, and dried in the sun. They can also be dried in a food dehydrator. Once dry, they may be ground into powders of varying fineness for use in sauces.

Recommended Varieties

'Anaheim M'. Mild, 8-inch pods.
SEED SOURCES: Liberty, Plants/Southwest, Rocky Mountain, Shepherd's

'Anaheim TMR 23'. Mild, 8-inch pods that are mosaic-resistant.
SEED SOURCES: Burpee, Gurney, Nichols, Park, Rocky Mountain, Tomato Grower's, Twilley

'Chimayó'. A land race from northern New Mexico with thin-walled, 6-inch pods. Medium heat.
SEED SOURCES: Enchanted Seeds, Native Seeds, Plants/Southwest

'Española Improved'. Medium heat, 5- to 6-inch pods.
SEED SOURCES: Enchanted Seeds, Old Southwest, Plants/Southwest, Rocky Mountain, Seeds of Change

'Fresno'. Erect, 2-inch pods, medium-hot.
SEED SOURCE: Seeds of Change

'New Mexico No. 6-4'. The most commonly grown New Mexican variety. Pods are 7 inches long, medium heat.
SEED SOURCES: Enchanted Seeds, Old Southwest, Plants/Southwest

'NuMex Big Jim'. Long pods up to 12 inches, medium heat.
SEED SOURCES: Enchanted Seeds, Gurney, Old Southwest, Plants/Southwest, Porter, Rocky Mountain, Westwind

'NuMex Eclipse'. Chocolate brown, mild, 5-inch pods, grown as an ornamental but can be eaten.
SEED SOURCE: Enchanted Seeds

'NuMex Joe E. Parker'. Improved 6-4 variety.
SEED SOURCES: Enchanted Seeds, Old Southwest, Shepherd's

'NuMex R Naky'. Pods are 5 to 7 inches long with mild heat.
SEED SOURCES: Enchanted Seeds, Plants/Southwest, Porter, Westwind

'NuMex Sunrise'. Bright yellow, mild, 5-inch pods, grown as an ornamental but can be eaten.

SEED SOURCES: Enchanted Seeds, Tomato Grower's

'NuMex Sunset'. Orange, mild, 5-inch pods, grown as an ornamental but can be eaten.

SEED SOURCES: Enchanted Seeds, Tomato Grower's

'Sandía'. Medium-hot, 6-inch pods with thin walls.

SEED SOURCES: Enchanted Seeds, Native Seeds, Old Southwest, Plants/Southwest, Rocky Mountain

Ornamentals

Although edible, Ornamentals are grown primarily for their unusual pod shapes or for their dense foliage and colorful, erect fruits. Many of the other types listed in this chapter, such as the Exotics and the Piquins, can be used as Ornamentals.

The Plant

Many Ornamentals have multiple stems and a compact habit. They seldom grow over 12 inches high. In low-light situations, some Ornamentals adopt a vinelike habit. The leaves are 1 to 2 inches long and ½ to 1 inch wide.

Flowers and Pods

The flower corollas are white with no spots. The pods vary greatly in shape, from small, Piquin-like pods to extremely long and thin Cayenne-like pods. In between, they can assume nearly any shape imaginable. The pods also vary greatly in heat, ranging between 0 and 50,000 Scoville Heat Units.

Cultivation

One distinguishing factor of Ornamentals is their ability to live in pots as perennials. In the garden, they often grow larger.

Use

Ornamentals are used for decoration, but they can be pickled or dried.

Recommended Varieties

'Black Plum'. Small, erect, dark purple, hot pods.
SEED SOURCES: Alfrey, Pepper Gal

'Bolivian Rainbow'. Purple foliage; stems, flowers, and pods that turn orange and red; very hot.
SEED SOURCE: Seeds of Change

'Christmas Ornamental Hot'. Purple pods turn red.
SEED SOURCES: Pepper Gal, Porter

'Fiesta Hot'. Compact plant with slender, red, 2-inch pods.
SEED SOURCES: Pepper Gal, Porter

'Fips'. Very small plants with conical, erect, red pods.
SEED SOURCES: Pepper Gal, Porter

'Firecracker'. Purple stems and flowers on 3-foot plant with 1-inch purple pods that turn red.
SEED SOURCE: Shepherd's

'Goat Horn Hot'. Curled and twisted, 3-inch pods.
SEED SOURCE: Sunrise

'Grandma's Home Pepper'. Small Siberian plant with erect, hot pods, able to endure low-light conditions.
SEED SOURCE: Harris

'Jigsaw'. Small, hot, red pods on small plants with attractive, variegated foliage.
SEED SOURCE: Enchanted Seeds

'NuMex Centennial'. Small, erect pods ranging in color from purple to cream to red. Hot.
SEED SOURCES: Enchanted Seeds, Old Southwest

'NuMex Twilight'. Purple, yellow, and red pods, small and hot.
SEED SOURCE: Enchanted Seeds

2.11 'Peter Peppers'

'Ordoño'. Orange, purple, and red 1-inch, erect, hot fruits.
SEED SOURCE: Native Seeds

'Peruvian Purple'. Purple foliage, stems, flowers, and pods; mildly hot.
SEED SOURCE: Seeds of Change

'Peter Pepper'. Mild pods resembling a human penis.
SEED SOURCES: Alfrey, Pepper Gal

'Spur Pepper'. Erect, 2-inch, very hot pods.
SEED SOURCES: Pepper Gal, Sunrise

'Super Chili'. Hybrid with 2½-inch, erect, cone-shaped, hot pods.
SEED SOURCES: Burpee, Field's, Gurney, Hastings, Liberty, Nichols, Park, Porter, Shepherd's, Tomato Grower's, Twilley

'Sweet Pickle'. Oval, erect, 2-inch fruits with no heat.
SEED SOURCE: Park

Paprika

In the United States, paprika is a spice, not a pod type. It is produced from any sweet, brilliantly red pepper. In Europe, there are distinct varieties of pepper called Paprika, which may or may not be pungent. What follows is a description of Hungarian varieties, some of which are available to growers in the United States.

2.12   European Paprika

The Plant

European Paprika varieties have an erect, multibranching habit with an intermediate number of stems. The plant varies in height between 10 and 30 inches. The leaves are ovate or lanceolate, medium green, and vary considerably in size depending upon variety.

Flowers and Pods

The flower corollas are white with no spots. The pods range in size and shape from small, flattened globes to pods that resemble those of the New Mexican varieties. They are pendant, thin-walled, pale yellow in immaturity, maturing to dark red. The pungency varies from 0 Scoville Heat Units for U.S. varieties to about 2,500 for European varieties.

Cultivation

Cultivation for the European types is similar to that of Bell peppers; for the U.S. varieties it is similar to that of the New Mexican pod type.

Use

The pods are dried and ground into powder.

Recommended European Varieties

'Alma Paprika'. A hot Hungarian variety with white pods turning red.
SEED SOURCE: Redwood City Seed

'Hungarian'. Red color, mildly hot, 3- to 4-inch pods.
SEED SOURCE: Enchanted Seeds

'Papri Mild'. Long, slender, 6-inch pods, mildly pungent.
SEED SOURCES: Porter, Seeds of Change

Pasilla

The name means "little raisin" in Spanish, an allusion to the dark brown color and raisinlike aroma of the dried pod. The produce industry in California confusingly refers to the dried Ancho chile as Pasilla.

The Plant

The Pasilla has an intermediate number of stems and an erect habit. It grows up to 3 feet high. The leaves are ovate, smooth, and medium green, about 3 inches long and 1½ inches wide.

Flowers and Pods

The flower corollas are white with no spots. The pods are elongate, cylindrical, furrowed, and measure between 6 and 12 inches long and 1 inch wide. They are very dark green, maturing to dark brown. Pasillas are fairly mild, measuring 1,000 to 1,500 Scoville Heat Units.

2.13 Pasilla

Cultivation

Most Pasillas are grown in Mexico; they are fairly uncommon in the home garden in the United States. The growing period is ninety days or more, and the plant can produce twenty or more pods. The pods should be allowed to dry on the plant.

Use

The green pods, called *chilaca*, can be used in the same manner as the New Mexican varieties. The dried pods are one of the main chiles used in *mole* sauces.

Recommended Varieties

'Pasilla' (generic). Medium-hot pods mature to dark brown.
   SEED SOURCES: Native Seeds, Old Southwest

'Apaseo'. Pods to 12 inches long, mildly hot.
  SEED SOURCE: Enchanted Seeds

'Salvatierra'. Mildly hot, 6- to 8-inch pods.
  SEED SOURCE: Enchanted Seeds

Pimiento

We use the Spanish spelling of this type to avoid confusion with the spice known as pimento, or allspice (*Pimenta dioica*).

The Plant

Pimientos are multistemmed with a habit that is subcompact tending toward prostrate, growing between 1 and 2½ feet tall. The leaves are medium green, ovate to lanceolate, smooth, and measure about 3 inches long and 1½ inches wide.

Flowers and Pods

The flower corollas are white with no spots. The pendant, heart-shaped, and thick-fleshed pods measure 2 to 4½ inches long and 2 to 3½ inches wide. The pods are dark green, maturing to bright red. They have no heat.

Cultivation

Pimientos are very similar to Bells in growing habit, and do well in home gardens, particularly in the South. The growing period is at least seventy-five days and the yield is ten pods per plant.

Use

Pimientos are often canned and are the familiar stuffing for olives. They are also used fresh in salads and are pickled. Some varieties are grown and dried for their powder, which is marketed in the United States as paprika. (One can also buy imported Hungarian paprika, which is made from the Paprika pepper.)

2.14　Pimiento

Recommended Varieties

'Pimiento' (generic).
　　SEED SOURCES: Enchanted Seeds, Field's, Hastings, Liberty, Nichols, Pinetree, Rocky Mountain, Tomato Grower's

'Pimento Select'. Heart-shaped, deep red pods, no heat.
　　SEED SOURCES: Field's, Hudson

'Pimiento Sweet'. Bright red pods with no heat.
　　SEED SOURCE: Porter

'Red Heart Pimiento'. Large, thick, heart-shaped pods with no heat.
　　SEED SOURCE: Seeds of Change

Piquin

The name of this type probably comes from the Spanish *pequeño,* meaning "small." The Piquins are also known by common names such as bird pepper and *chile mosquito.* Most are unnamed varieties, both wild and domesticated, varying in pod size and shape from BBs to de Arbol–like fruits. Generally speaking, the wild varieties (spherical *tepins*) are called *chiltepins* and the domesticated varieties (oblong *piquins*) are called Piquins or Pequins, but in Texas the wild varieties are called *chilipiquins.*

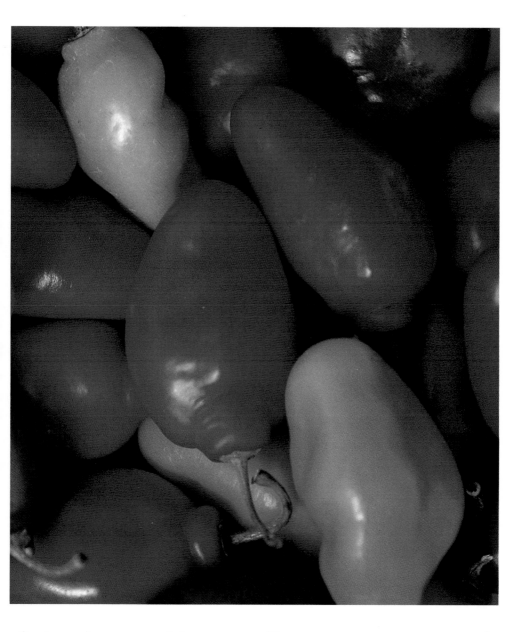

Capsicum pubescens, commonly known as *rocoto*. These peppers start out green, mature to red or yellow, and are the only peppers with black seeds. (Photo by Paul W. Bosland.)

The flower of the *rocoto* (*Capsicum pubescens*) is a distinctive purple. The glistening drops you can see at the center are nectar we placed there to attract insects for cross-pollination. (Photo by Paul W. Bosland.)

Known as "puppy peppers," these very attractive, nonpungent peppers are common in Costa Rica. Seeds for unusual varieties such as this may be available through Seed Savers Exchange (see Resources). (Photo by Dave DeWitt.)

Capsicum tovarii, a wild species from South America. Note the small fruits, typical of virtually all wild species. They attract birds, who eat them and spread the seeds, which ensures the pepper's survival. (Photo by Paul W. Bosland.)

The Plant

Piquins usually have an intermediate number of stems and an erect habit, but they can vary greatly. In the wild, Piquins can grow 6 feet high or more, and in the greenhouse they have grown 15 feet high in one season. Some varieties have a prostrate habit, spreading across the ground like a ground cover. The leaves are medium green and are lanceolate or ovate, measuring about 3½ inches long by 1½ inches wide.

Flowers and Pods

The flower corollas are white with no spots. The pods are borne erect, are round or oblong, and measure between ¼ and ½ inch in both length and width. Domesticated varieties usually have elongate, pointed pods, usually borne erect but occasionally pendant, sometimes measuring up to 2 inches long. Piquins are extremely hot, measuring between 50,000 and 100,000 Scoville Heat Units.

Cultivation

Piquins do well in the home garden and are particularly suited to being grown in containers as perennials. Paul Bessey, the garden

2.15   *Chiltepins*

51

writer of the *Arizona Daily Star,* reports that rosy-headed house finches regularly decimate his ripening *chiltepins,* so some netting protection from birds may be necessary. The growing period is at least ninety days, and the plant can produce between fifty and one hundred pods, depending on its size and growing period.

Use

The pods are collected and dried. They can be ground into powder or made into extremely hot sauces, but are most commonly crushed into soups, stews, and bean dishes.

Recommended Varieties

'*Chiltepin*' (generic). Small, round to slightly pointed pods, extremely hot.
   SEED SOURCES: Native Seeds, Plants/Southwest, Seeds of Change

'Hermosillo Select'. A *chiltepin* from Sonora with large spherical pods.
   SEED SOURCE: Native Seeds

'NuMex Bailey Piquin'. Very hot, ¾ inch long and ¼ inch wide.
   SEED SOURCES: Enchanted Seeds, Old Southwest

'Texas'. A *chiltepin* from Wimberly, west of Austin.
   SEED SOURCE: Native Seeds

Serrano

The Serrano is the best chile for fresh salsas. Its name means "from the mountains," because it was first grown in the mountains of northern Puebla and Hidalgo in Mexico.

The Plant

Serranos vary in habit from compact to erect, have an intermediate number of stems, and grow 1½ to 5 feet high. The leaves vary from light to dark green, are pubescent (hairy), and measure 3½ to 5 inches long and 1½ to 2 inches wide.

2.16   Serrano

Flowers and Pods

The flower corollas are white with no spots. The pods grow erect or pendant, are bluntly pointed, and measure 1 to 4 inches long and ½ inch wide. Serranos measure between 10,000 and 20,000 Scoville Heat Units.

Cultivation

Serranos, grown extensively in Mexico, grow and fruit well in the home garden. The growing period is at least ninety days. The plant can produce up to fifty pods.

Use

"These hot varieties are often eaten raw by native Mexicans, as are radishes," wrote H. C. Irish in 1930. In Mexico, 90 percent of the crop is used fresh and the rest is canned. Serranos are most commonly used in fresh, *pico de gallo*–type salsas.

Recommended Varieties

'Serrano' (generic). Small, hot pods.
SEED SOURCES: Burpee, Enchanted Seeds, Gurney, Plants/Southwest, Porter, Redwood City Seed, Rocky Mountain, Seeds of Change, Territorial Seed, Tomato Grower's

'TAM Hidalgo'. Mildly pungent.
SEED SOURCES: Porter, Rocky Mountain

Squash

Also called Cheese or Tomato peppers, the Squash type is best known for the flattened shape of the pods. Some experts believe that the Bell type was developed from Squash peppers.

The Plant

Most plants of the Squash type are multistemmed with a habit that is subcompact tending toward prostrate, growing 1 to 2½ feet tall. The leaves are medium green, ovate to lanceolate, smooth, and measure about 3 inches long and 1½ inches wide.

Flowers and Pods

The flower corollas are white with no spots. The flattened pods have a squashlike shape and measure about 1 inch long and 2 inches wide. They are not usually pungent, but some hot varieties are now available. The pods are green or yellow, turning red at maturity.

Cultivation

The Squash type, uncommon in home gardens, is grown just like the Bells.

Use

Squash peppers are cultivated commercially and dried for paprika. Their oleoresins are extracted and used as coloring agents in

2.17 Squash

various foods. When grown at home, squash peppers are most often used in salads or as an attractive garnish.

Recommended Varieties

'Squash' (generic). Flattened pods.
   SEED SOURCE: Alfrey

'Red Squash Hot'. Very hot, red, patty-pan pods.
   SEED SOURCE: Porter

'Yellow Squash Hot'. Golden yellow, 2-inch, hot pods.
   SEED SOURCE: Porter

Wax

The shiny appearance of the pods is the reason the type is called Wax. They vary greatly in size, shape, and pungency.

The Plant

Wax peppers have multiple stems and a compact habit, growing up to 30 inches high. The leaves are ovate, medium green, and up to 5 inches long and 3 inches wide.

2.18   Wax

Flowers and Pods

The flower corollas are white with no spots. The pods vary greatly in size and shape, from the small, 2-inch 'Caloro' to the giant 'Banana Supreme' with its 8-inch pods. Generally speaking, the small pods are borne erect and the long ones pendant. The pods are conical but tapering, and bluntly pointed at the end. Yield is twenty-five or more pods per plant, and the heat scale varies from 0 to 40,000 Scoville Heat Units.

Cultivation

Most Wax varieties are very prolific in the home garden, fruiting early and producing well. The growing season is seventy or more days.

Use

The milder Wax varieties can be used fresh in salads. All varieties can be pickled, which is the most common use of commercially grown Wax peppers.

Recommended Varieties

'Banana Supreme'. Hybrid with 8-inch, yellow pods and no heat.
    SEED SOURCES: Tomato Grower's, Twilley

'Caloro'. Yellow-orange, medium-hot, 2-inch pods.
SEED SOURCE: Rocky Mountain

'Gold Spike'. Hybrid, very hot, 2½-inch pods.
SEED SOURCE: Porter

'Hungarian Rainbow Wax'. Multicolored, hot pods.
SEED SOURCE: Liberty

'Hungarian Yellow Wax Hot'. Medium-hot, 6-inch pods.
SEED SOURCES: Burpee, Gurney, Harris, High Altitude, Johnny's, Liberty, Park, Porter, Rocky Mountain, Seeds of Change, Territorial Seed, Twilley

'Santa Fe Grande'. Short, thick, yellow pods good for pickling, medium heat.
SEED SOURCES: Plants/Southwest, Redwood City Seed, Rocky Mountain, Seeds of Change, Seeds West, Westwind

'Sweet Banana'. Six-inch pods, yellow turning red, with no heat.
SEED SOURCES: Burpee, Enchanted Seeds, Gurney, Harris, Hastings, Liberty, Park, Pinetree, Porter, Rocky Mountain, Tomato Grower's, Twilley, Westwind

CHAPTER 3

Other Species and Pod Types

In addition to the *annuums*, there are four other species of domesticated capsicums: *baccatum, chinense, frutescens,* and *pubescens.* By far the most familiar of these species is *frutescens,* which includes the Tabasco pepper, from which the famous sauce is made. Recently, the *chinense* species has become popular because of the Habanero type, which has the highest heat level of any capsicum. Because their seed has only recently become commercially available, the *baccatum* and *pubescens* species are just becoming known to home gardeners.

Capsicum baccatum

The *baccatum* species, familiarly termed *ají* throughout South America, originated either in Bolivia or in Peru and, according to archaeological evidence, was probably domesticated in Peru about 2,500 B.C. Extensive *baccatum* material found at the Huaca Prieta archaeological site shows that the species was gradually improved by the pre-Incan civilizations. The size of the fruit increased and the fruits gradually became nondeciduous and stayed on the plants until they were ripe. There are two wild forms (varieties *baccatum* and *microcarpum*) and a domesticated form (variety *pendulum*). The pods of the domesticated form are diverse in shape and size, ranging from short, pointed pods borne erect to long, pendant pods resembling those of the New Mexican varieties. The *baccatum* species is generally distinguished from the other species by the yellow, green, or tan spots on the corollas, and by the yellow anthers.

Baccatums are cultivated in Argentina, Colombia, Ecuador,

3.1 Pod Variations in *C. baccatum*

Peru, Brazil, and Bolivia, and the species has been introduced into Costa Rica, India, and the United States. In the United States, it is grown and packed commercially to a very limited extent in California under the brand name Mild Italian and in Nevada under the brand name Chileno.

The Plant

The *baccatums* are tall, sometimes reaching 5 feet, have multiple stems and an erect habit, occasionally tending toward sprawling. The large, dark green leaves measure up to 7 inches long and 4 inches wide.

Flowers and Pods

The flower corollas are white with distinctive dark green or brown spots; anthers are yellow or tan. The pods usually begin erect and become pendant as they mature, are elongate in shape, and measure 3 to 6 inches long and ¾ to 1½ inches wide. They usually mature to an orange-red, but yellow and brown colors also appear in some varieties. The pods measure between 30,000 and 50,000 Scoville Heat Units.

Cultivation

The *baccatum* plants tend to stand out in the garden like small trees. Their growing period is 120 days or more, and the plants can produce forty or more pods.

Use

The pods have a distinctive, fruity flavor and are used fresh in *ceviche* (lime-marinated fish) in South America. They can also be used in fresh salsas, and the pods are easily dried and ground into colorful powders.

Recommended Varieties

'Ají' (generic). Orange-red, 3- to 5-inch pods, very hot.
  SEED SOURCE: Enchanted Seeds

'Ají Amarillo'. Bright yellow, 2- to 3-inch pods, very hot.
  SEED SOURCE: Enchanted Seeds

Capsicum chinense

This entire species is often referred to as "Habanero," but that appellation is a misnomer because there are literally hundreds of pod types, and the name Habanero refers to a specific pod type from the Yucatán Peninsula of Mexico.

The Amazon basin was the center of origin for the *chinense* species, famous for having the hottest peppers of them all. The oldest known *chinense* is the sixty-five-hundred-year-old pod found intact in Guitarrero Cave in Peru.

Bernabe Cobo, a naturalist who traveled throughout South America during the early seventeenth century, was probably the first European to study the *chinense* species. He estimated that there were at least forty different varieties of these chiles, "some as large as limes or large plums; others, as small as pine nuts or even grains of wheat, and between the two extremes are many different sizes. No less variety is found in color . . . and the same difference is found in form and shape."

Chinense is the most important cultivated pepper east of the Andes in South America. There is a great diversity of pod shape and heat levels ranging from 0 to 300,000 Scoville Heat Units. At some point, indigenous peoples transferred the *chinense* from the Amazon Basin into the Caribbean, where land races developed on nearly every island. Today, most countries in the Caribbean and Central and South America have a local variety, and, of course, each has a common name. *Chinense* is called "goat pepper" in the Bahamas, "Scotch bonnet" in Jamaica, "Congo pepper" in Trinidad, "*pimenta de cheiro*" in Brazil, "*chombo*" in Panama, and "Panama" in Costa Rica. The wild *chinense* varieties have numerous local names in Spanish, Portuguese, and Indian dialects that may be translated as "fish eye," "parakeet's eye," and "blowgun pepper."

In the Yucatán Peninsula the *chinense* is called "Habanero," which means "from Havana," hinting of a transference to Mexico from the Caribbean. It long has been rumored that Habaneros no longer grow in Cuba, but in 1990 Richard Rice, a pepper aficionado, sent us seeds given to him by Cuban refugees. The seeds did indeed produce Habaneros, proving that they are still grown in Cuba today. The species was transferred to Africa during the colonization of Brazil or during the later traffic in slaves, and today there are many *chinense* varieties in Africa.

Today, Habaneros are grown commercially in the Yucatán Peninsula of Mexico, where about fifteen hundred tons a year are harvested. They are cultivated to a lesser extent in Belize, and there are small commercial fields of other *chinense* varieties in Jamaica, Trinidad, and to a limited extent on other islands, among them the Bahamas. In Costa Rica, a variety of *chinense* called 'Rica Red', developed by Stuart Jeffrey and Cody Jordan of Quetzál Foods, is grown commercially; about two hundred acres were under cultivation in 1992. In the United States, there are two significant commercial growing operations: one in California and the other in the Texas Hill Country. The 'Datil' pepper, a *chinense* variety grown for about three hundred years in St. Augustine, Florida, is processed into sauces and jellies, but growers there jealously protect their seeds and none are available commercially. Varieties have been developed and named in Mexico, but are not commercially available to home gardeners. In the United States, most commercially available Habanero seeds are generic.

Interestingly enough, in the Amazon region of Brazil, mildly pungent *chinense* varieties have been crossed with Bell peppers to produce sweet hybrids that, under the hot and humid conditions there, are more disease resistant than *annuums*. S. S. Cheng, the researcher responsible for the experiment, notes: "The advantages of *C. chinense* cultivation are the longer harvest periods, no pesticide application requirement, and low production cost. A breeding program is under way to transfer fruit quality from *C. annuum* to *C. chinense*."

The Plant

Chinense varieties range between 1 and 4½ feet tall, depending on environmental factors. Some perennial varieties have grown as tall as 8 feet in tropical climates, but the average height in the U.S. garden is about 2 feet. It has multiple stems and an erect habit. The leaves are pale to medium green, large and wrinkled, reaching 6 inches long and 4 inches wide.

Flowers and Pods

The flowers have white to greenish white corollas and purple anthers and filaments. The plant sets between 2 and 6 fruits per node. The pods are pendant and campanulate (a flattened bell shape). Some are elongate and pointed at the end; others are flattened at the end and resemble a tam, or bonnet. They are usually about 2½ inches long and 1 to 2 inches wide, green when immature and maturing to red, orange, yellow, or white. Although the *chinense* range in heat from 0 to 250,000 (the hottest ever measured), they average between 80,000 and 150,000 Scoville Heat Units.

Cultivation

The seeds tend to take a long time to germinate. The *chinense*, being tropical plants, do best in areas with high humidity and warm nights. They are slow growers, especially in the Southwest, and the growing period is between 80 and 120 days or more. Gardening writer Rosalind Creasy reports that she has success with Habaneros

3.2   Pod Variations in *C. chinense*

in Northern California. The yield varies enormously according to how well the particular plants adapt to the local environment; in New Mexico we have grown stunted plants with as few as ten pods and large, bushy plants with fifty or more.

Use

The *chinense* varieties have an unmistakable, fruity aroma and taste that some people describe as apricotlike. The pods are used fresh in salsas, and are commonly combined with carrots and onions to make very hot, liquid sauces. They can be dried and ground into powder, but be sure to wear a protective mask while grinding them.

Recommended Varieties

'Habanero' (generic).
    SEED SOURCES: Enchanted Seeds, Liberty, Nichols, Plants/Southwest, Porter, Redwood City Seed, Rocky Mountain, Shepherd's, Tomato Grower's, Westwind

'Rica Red'. Large pods from Costa Rica, maturing to red.
    SEED SOURCE: Old Southwest

Capsicum frutescens

The Tabasco is the most recognizable variety of this species, known from the famous sauce that is now more than 125 years old. Another famous variety is the *malagueta*, which grows wild in the Amazon basin in Brazil, where the species probably originated. Curiously, there are not as many names for the wild varieties as there are for some other species. The most common name is bird pepper. No domesticated *frutescens* has ever been found in an archaeological site in Middle or South America, but ethnobotanists speculate that the domestication site was probably Panama and from there it spread to Mexico and the Caribbean.

At any rate, we know that the Tabasco variety of *frutescens* was being cultivated near Tabasco, Mexico, in the early 1840s because it was transferred to Louisiana in 1848, where it was eventually grown to produce Tabasco sauce. Demand outstripped supply, and today Tabascos are commercially grown in Central America and Colombia and shipped in mash form to Louisiana.

In Louisiana, Tabasco peppers fell victim to the tobacco etch virus (TEV), but were rescued in 1970 with the introduction of 'Greenleaf Tabasco,' a TEV-resistant variety. Today at Avery Island, the site of the original Tabasco growing and manufacturing operation, there are still fields of Tabasco under cultivation—but mostly for crop improvement and seed production.

Some varieties of *frutescens* found their way to India and the Far East, where they are still called bird pepper. There they are cultivated to make hot sauces and curries.

3.3 The *malagueta* from Brazil

The Plant

Tabasco plants have a compact habit, an intermediate number of stems, and grow 1 to 4 feet high, depending on climate and growing conditions. The leaves are ovate, smooth, and measure 2½ inches long and 2½ inches wide.

Flowers and Pods

The flowers have greenish white corollas with no spots and blue anthers. The pods are borne erect and measure up to 1½ inches long and ⅜ inch wide. Immature pods are yellow or green, maturing to bright red. Tabascos are quite hot, measuring between 30,000 and 50,000 Scoville Heat Units.

Cultivation

The height of the plants depends on climate, with the plants growing the largest in warmer parts of the country. The plant is particularly good for container gardening. One of our specimens lived as a perennial for four years in a pot, but gradually lost vigor and produced fewer pods each year. A single plant can produce one hundred or more pods.

Use

The most common use for the pods is in hot sauces; they are crushed, salted, fermented, and combined with vinegar. The pods can, however, be used fresh in salsas and can be dried for adding to stir-fry dishes.

Recommended Varieties

'Tabasco' (generic). Yellow and red, erect, very hot pods.
SEED SOURCES: Enchanted Seeds, Porter, Redwood City Seed, Tomato Grower's

'Greenleaf Tabasco'. Resistant to tobacco etch virus, heavy yields.
SEED SOURCES: Enchanted Seeds, Hastings

Capsicum pubescens

Pubescens is the only domesticated species with no wild form; two wild species, *C. cardenasii* and *C. eximium*, are closely related. The center of origin for this species was Bolivia, and according to botanist Charles Heiser it was probably domesticated about 6,000 B.C., making it one of the oldest domesticated plants in the Americas. Heiser, citing Garcilaso de la Vega (1609), notes that *pubescens* was "the most common pepper among the Incas, just as it is today in Cuzco, the former capital of the Incan empire." It is grown today in the Andes from Bolivia to Colombia, mostly in small family plots. It is also cultivated in highland areas of Central America and Mexico.

The common name for this species in South America is *rocoto*. In Mexico, it may also be called *chile manzano* (apple pepper), and *chile perón* (pear pepper), allusions to its varying, fruitlike shapes. In some parts of Mexico and Guatemala, *pubescens* are called *chile caballo*, horse pepper. Yellow *pubescens* are called *canarios*, or canaries, in parts of Mexico, particularly Oaxaca.

The Plant

Pubescens has a compact to erect habit, although sometimes it sprawls. It grows up to 4 feet tall, but 2 feet is more usual in U.S. gardens. The leaves are ovate, light to dark green, very pubescent (hairy), and measure up to 3½ inches long and 2 inches wide.

Flowers and Pods

The flowers have purple corollas, purple anthers, and stand erect above the leaves. The pods are round, sometimes pear-shaped. They measure about 2 to 3 inches long and 2 to 2½ inches wide, but some pods as large as Bell peppers have been reported. The pods are green in their immature state, maturing to yellow, orange, or red. Their heat level is between 30,000 and 60,000 Scoville Heat Units. The *pubescens* varieties contain a unique set of capsaicinoids (pungency compounds), causing some people to believe they are hotter than Habaneros. In parts of the Americas they are described as *el más picante de los picantes*, "the hottest of the hot."

3.4   Rocoto

Cultivation

The *pubescens* are traditionally grown in high mountain areas of tropical countries. They can survive very light frosts but not hard freezes. Some sources state that, because of their long growing season and need for long day-length, the *pubescens* varieties are unsuitable for cultivation in the United States. Our experiments have shown, however, that plants started early will fruit in one season. Charlie Ward of Virginia Beach, Virginia, reported that he has the best results when he grows his *rocotos* for twenty-two months. For the first year he raises them in pots and then transplants them into the garden for the second year. Despite the fact that the elevation of his garden is a mere ten feet above sea level, his *rocotos* "grew like weeds" the second year and produced many large, apple-shaped, red and yellow pods. Some plants may not fruit because there is self-incompatibility in the species. To set fruit, pollen must be transferred by bees or humans from a neighboring plant. The species also responds well when shaded because the foliage has a tendency to burn in full sun. The growing season is long, 120 days or more, and the plants produce up to thirty pods, depending on the length of the growing season.

Transplanted *rocotos* that were grown in fields at Las Cruces, New Mexico, burned up in the sun. Shading helped, but by the time the plants set fruit, a frost killed them. In Albuquerque, which is cooler, shaded *rocotos* did fairly well, with up to ten pods per plant.

Use

Pubescens varieties are usually eaten fresh because the pods are so thick they are difficult to dry. They are commonly used in fresh salsas, and the larger pods can be stuffed with meat or cheese and baked.

Recommended Varieties

'Rocoto' (generic). Very hot, thick-walled pods that mature to red.
SEED SOURCES: Enchanted Seeds, Redwood City Seed

'Manzano Amarillo'. Bright yellow pods, very hot.
SEED SOURCE: Hudson

'Manzano Rojo'. Dark red pods, very hot.
SEED SOURCE: Hudson

CHAPTER 4

Preparing the Garden

Pepper gardeners should always plan before they plant. The planning involves many elements: the varieties of peppers to be grown, other vegetables and herbs in the garden, the type of garden, and the preparation of the garden before planting.

Selecting the Right Varieties

A large number of pepper varieties are available to the home gardener. Choosing the best varieties to grow in the garden is important. Seed companies and state college experiment stations devote tremendous effort to the development of disease-resistant, highly productive varieties that are tailor-made for different climates. Some of these new varieties may be better than the ones gardeners traditionally grow.

In the winter, when planning the garden, write for the seed catalogs offered by the companies listed in the Resources. Catalogs offer a far wider choice of varieties than do seed displays at local nurseries and retail shops. Seed catalogs are also the most dependable source of new varieties, and many of the seed companies offer what they call "proprietary cultivars," varieties that are sold exclusively by one company. Often, these proprietary cultivars are hybrids, first-generation crosses that must be hand-pollinated each year. Seed catalogs also offer better access to the All-America Selections, which are varieties chosen by experts as the all-around best.

According to the seed companies, all the varieties grow well everywhere. This is just not true. For example, the New Mexican varieties grow well in the Southwest but not that well in the Northwest and Northeast. Bells and Habaneros do not grow as well in the Southwest as they do in other regions.

To decide which varieties to plant, consult gardening neighbors, a local gardening club, or the county agricultural or extension agent. Or, learn from experience. When reading the variety description on the seed packet or in the catalog, look for the qualities that are most important, such as growing period, yield, disease resistance, and recommendations for climatic zones. As mentioned in chapters 2 and 3, some varieties are best suited for pickling, some for drying, some for fresh use, and some for processing and freezing.

A variety that performs well in one region may be unsuitable in another because of a susceptibility to disease or a particular maturity date. It is, however, difficult to persuade dedicated pepper growers not to grow a specific variety. Even if you know that the soil conditions and climate are wrong, use some of the hints in later chapters of this book; you may be successful. You can modify the microclimate in your garden. For example, in the Southwest, Habaneros that have been shaded generally yield better. Peppers that are susceptible to root rot can be saved if you create a scree in the garden to improve drainage.

Some basic tips will make pepper gardening more enjoyable. In many climates, the variety makes the difference between a bumper harvest and outright failure. In the Southeast and Midwest, where summer rains are common, peppers that are resistant to bacterial leaf spot should be grown. Because this disease is caused by a bacterium, it cannot be controlled by chemicals, so the best and most effective way to ensure a bountiful harvest is to plant resistant varieties. Catalogs and seed packets describe the resistance factors of the varieties.

The early or late maturity of a variety is also a very important consideration. At high altitudes or in cool climates, both with short growing seasons, peppers must be able to mature and set fruit rapidly. Early maturing varieties are valuable to the cool-climate gardener who might not be able to mature the late cultivars at all because of their heat requirements, and to the hot-climate gardener who wants an early harvest.

The growing period, the number of days from sowing the seed to maturity (listed in catalogs and on seed packets), is an important clue for the gardener. The number of days listed in the growing period is, however, based upon ideal conditions. In some cases, the growing period means the number of days from *transplanting* to pod *picking*. A Bell pepper listed to mature in sixty days may well do that in Davis, California, in the warm Sacramento Valley. But that same pepper may require eighty days to mature in Corvallis, Oregon, or one hundred days in Seattle, Washington.

Knowing even the approximate growing period can be useful to gardeners in hot climates, who can plant early varieties at the beginning of the season so that they can be harvested before the really hot weather arrives. And an early, sixty-day pepper, planted under plastic tunnels in California or Florida in December or January, will mature in March. If this same variety is planted in late spring, it might mature in fifty days or fewer, but the plant will be underdeveloped and the pods small and sunburned.

Many new varieties of peppers are hybrids that are superior to the older variety of the same or similar name. Hybrid varieties are often resistant to one or more diseases, grow rapidly, and produce more uniform pods than the older variety does. Hybrids usually cost more, but for most gardeners, and especially for organic gardeners who eschew pesticides, the disease resistance alone is worth the additional cost. Hybrids do not reproduce true to type because they are only first-generation crosses, so saving seed is not worthwhile.

Here are some hints about how to choose the varieties to grow. First, know your own needs. John and Ann Swan of Westchester, Pennsylvania, put it this way: "Before we order seeds, we decide how many fruits of each variety we will need to grow for our own kitchen and for the Pennsylvania Horticultural Society's Harvest Show. Then we project how many plants we will need to produce that number. Finally, we add a few varieties that we've never grown before."

Keep records about the pepper garden. List the varieties planted and note those that performed well. Use a loose-leaf or bound notebook rather than individual notes, to prevent losing important information. Record the dates on which the seeds or seedlings were planted, how many pods were produced, and when they matured. Also record any disease problems, unusual weather, insect infestations, or any other observation that is significant. At the end of the growing season, these records can be reviewed and the best-performing varieties can be determined. By comparing the performance of the varieties, you can eliminate the poor ones and replace them with others the following year.

Other Plants in the Garden

Another important factor in choosing pepper varieties is the selection of accompanying plants in the garden. Because most people grow peppers to eat them, it makes sense to select other vegetables and herbs that blend harmoniously with peppers in meals, especially if peppers are a primary crop in the garden. Peppers are, of course, consumed by themselves in fresh or pickled form. But their most common use is in combination with other foods. An informal survey was conducted of books with collections of hot and spicy recipes to determine which vegetables and herbs are most commonly combined with peppers. Based on the results, gardeners might use the following list, along with their own tastes, to select the plants to accompany favorite peppers in the garden.

BASIL. An herb that adds flavor to hot and spicy Italian sauces, basil can be combined with fresh green chile peppers such as New Mexican, Serranos, and Jalapeños, to make powerful pestos. It also flavors stuffed Bell or Pimiento peppers.

BEANS. The combination of beans and peppers is traditional. Green beans are often seasoned, but the most common blend is pinto beans and the red pods or powders of Anchos, Pasillas, *chipotles*, or New Mexican varieties.

CARROTS. Carrots may be pickled with peppers, cooked with small hot peppers and dill, and used as a base for Habanero pepper sauces.

CAULIFLOWER. Used raw, cauliflower often accompanies peppers in pickled or marinated vegetable combinations.

CILANTRO. Also called coriander or Chinese parsley, this herb is the principal seasoning in fresh Mexican and Southwestern salsas. It combines well with Serranos, Jalapeños, Habaneros, and Piquins.

CORN. When processed into meal and then made into *tortillas*, corn with chile peppers is a traditional combination, appearing as *tacos* and *enchiladas*. Fresh corn is often cooked with green New Mexican varieties and is also used in fresh salsas.

CUMIN. The seeds of this spice are commonly used in Mexican and Southwestern cooked chile pepper sauces.

EGGPLANTS. Fellow members of the Solanaceae family, eggplants and peppers are often combined in casseroles.

GARLIC. Garlic is commonly combined with peppers in salsas, sauces, pickles, chutneys, salads, soups, and curries.

JÍCAMA. A favorite salad ingredient in the Southwest and Mexico, *jícama* is often sprinkled first with lime juice and then with red chile powder.

LETTUCE. Gardeners have fun growing various types of exotic lettuce and combining them in salads with Bell peppers, Pimientos, Cubans, and sometimes the hotter peppers.

ONIONS. Onions are probably the vegetable most commonly combined with peppers. They are used in sauces, salsas, salads, pickles, and casseroles.

OREGANO. Mexican oregano (*Lippia graveolens* and *L. palmeri*), is commonly combined with Mexican peppers in salsas, sauces, stews, soups, and combination dishes.

POTATOES. Another ancient combination, this time from South America, potatoes and peppers often appear together. Cooked potatoes are commonly topped with chile powders and sauces.

SPINACH. Like lettuce, spinach is combined with peppers in salads. It is also cooked with New Mexican varieties in dishes such as *quelites*.

SQUASH. Varieties of squash, such as zucchini and crookneck, are often cooked with fresh hot peppers. Winter squash and pumpkins are baked with chile powders.

TOMATILLOS. These small husk tomatoes are popular in the Southwest and Mexico. They are combined with fresh hot peppers such as Serranos and Jalapeños in salsas and sauces.

TOMATOES. Many different varieties of tomatoes may be used with peppers in salads, salsas, sauces, casseroles, and numerous combination dishes.

Garden Design and Planning

After choosing the varieties of peppers to plant, the gardener must plan the garden. Many considerations affect garden design, including site, soil type, rainfall, method of irrigation, mature height of various plants, structural support for plants such as pole beans and tomatoes, and access to the garden for weeding and harvesting. We will discuss the most commonly used pepper garden designs, and their benefits and drawbacks.

Ridges and Furrows

Perhaps the most familiar of all, this garden design consists of alternating ridges (or hills) and furrows (or trenches). The plants grow along the ridges and are irrigated from the furrows. This method works well for commercial growers who must use farm

4.1 **Ridges and Furrows**

equipment to plow, till, weed, and apply fertilizers and insecticides. The furrows are very handy for quick irrigating, too. Ridges and furrows are also useful in regions with heavy rainfall because the moisture tends to drain off the ridges and into the furrows.

For the home gardener the ridges-and-furrows design has some drawbacks. It wastes space, and plants cannot be packed efficiently into smaller gardens. In desert regions, the ridges tend to draw salts to their peaks and injure the plants. Unless proper mulch is used, the ridges tend to dry out quickly.

Flat Beds

Perhaps the simplest garden to construct is one made of flat beds. After soil preparation, the site is surrounded by a berm (a bank of raised soil) that will hold water during flood irrigation or after rain. The interior part of the flat bed is carefully leveled to avoid high spots, which would dry out too quickly. Flat beds should only be about four feet wide to allow easy access for weeding and harvesting.

Flat beds tend to hold water better and use space more efficiently than ridges and furrows do. Yields of peppers tend to be larger because more plants can fit into the available space. A disadvantage is the lack of access: without furrows, there are no walkways through the plants. Another disadvantage is that the necessity for level beds precludes their use on sloping sites.

4.2 Flat Beds

4.3   Raised Beds

Raised Beds

Used primarily for good drainage, raised beds are built up out of bricks, blocks, logs, or wood planks to contain the garden above the usual soil level. A well-drained soil mixture is poured into a huge container. This design is often used in damp climates or in places where the soil contains a lot of clay. There are a couple of drawbacks to this system: it can dry out quickly and the material retaining the beds must be maintained.

4.4   Sunken Beds

Sunken Beds

This design, used by the ancient Egyptians, is the opposite of ridges and furrows. The plants are placed in the furrows, where they are protected from high winds until they are well established. The disadvantage to this system is that the plants are placed where the most water accumulates, so the garden must be well drained.

Modified Irrigated Beds

After years of growing peppers in small plots in the Southwest, we have developed a system that works well because it allows us to grow peppers with most of the other vegetables and herbs mentioned above. It also maximizes space in a narrow garden, provides excellent access, and allows quick and efficient irrigation. Essentially, it combines elements of both ridges and furrows and flat beds, and can be used in gardens with a slight slope.

A brick, stone, or concrete walkway down the center of the garden allows easy access. In the plot on each side of the walkway, a shallow center furrow is cut to provide irrigation. From these center furrows, side furrows are cut, making slightly raised beds that are not

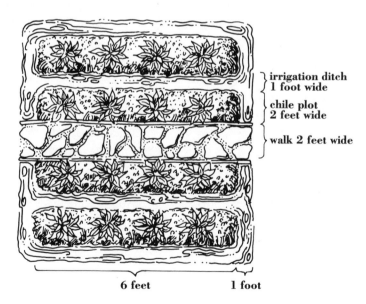

irrigation ditch
1 foot wide

chile plot
2 feet wide

walk 2 feet wide

6 feet   1 foot

4.5   Modified Irrigated Beds

as high as conventional ridges are. During irrigation, the small beds will be usually be surrounded by water on three sides. Irrigation is easy because the hose is placed at one end of each bed, and the furrows fill quickly. In sloping gardens the spread of water may be controlled with small dams made from soil or sections of two-by-fours.

This design will also work in wetter regions if the soil is well drained. (In extremely wet regions, a flat bed without furrows is better.) One drawback is that the walkway takes up a lot of space; however, it is relatively weed-free and can be used during irrigation.

After choosing the design of the pepper garden, the gardener should prepare a scale drawing and choose locations for the peppers and accompanying plants. The next steps involve improving the garden site. When care is taken to improve the soil and provide the best drainage possible, great pepper plants are usually the result.

Composting

The key to a successful pepper garden is the addition of compost, which improves workability, water-holding capability, drainage, and fertility of the soil. Some gardeners have no choice about composting because many landfills across the country do not accept organic yard refuse such as grass clippings. For them, composting is a necessity.

Composting is the process whereby organic material, with the help of microorganisms, insects, earthworms, and water, decomposes into humus. Also necessary is oxygen, for anaerobic decomposition is a slow process that causes foul odors.

Several books have been written on composting, which seems to indicate that the process is enormously complicated. Gardening writer Jack Ruttle points out that "people have been making compost for a thousand years, time enough for a considerable mythology to have arisen around the practice. Some of the methods for assuring a 'perfect' compost sound like pure witchcraft. Certainly, the idea of perfect compost, which has become the holy grail to some gardeners, discourages many others." In reality, composting is quite simple, and a compost pile should always be a part of pepper gardening.

Site Selection

A good compost pile must have ample available water, an inconspicuous location convenient to the garden, and at least six hours of sunlight a day.

Containers

A compost pile can be just that—a pile of organic material. Such piles are, however, sloppy and difficult to control, so most gardeners prefer to use containers or bins for composting. The simplest containers are holes or trenches in the ground, but the compost in them is difficult to turn and to remove.

Containers can be constructed from a wide variety of materials, including wire screening, wooden bins, cinder blocks or bricks without mortar, and snowfencing. They should all be enclosed on three sides, with the front and top open.

Some sources suggest that piles can be as large as ten feet long and five feet high, but such large piles are difficult to maintain. The ideal pile in a bin or container is three feet high by three feet wide. Anything larger is difficult to turn and tends to compact too much, preventing oxygen from reaching all parts of the pile. If you have too much organic material, start another pile.

Proper Materials

Coffee grounds, corn stalks and leaves, egg shells, garden plants killed by frost, grass clippings, kitchen scraps (fruits and vegetables), leaves, manure from herbivores, pine needles, sawdust, shredded newspaper, straw, and unseeded weeds all make good compost.

Bones, branches from trees and shrubs, colored newsprint, diseased garden plants, fats and grease, grass clippings treated with herbicides, kitty litter, magazine pages, manure from carnivores such as pets, meat, plastics, synthetic products, and wood ashes are *unacceptable* for compost.

It is important that dissimilar materials be added in layers. For example, the pile should not consist solely of grass clippings, which tend to pack together and prevent air circulation. Rather, the clippings should be interspersed with layers of other materials.

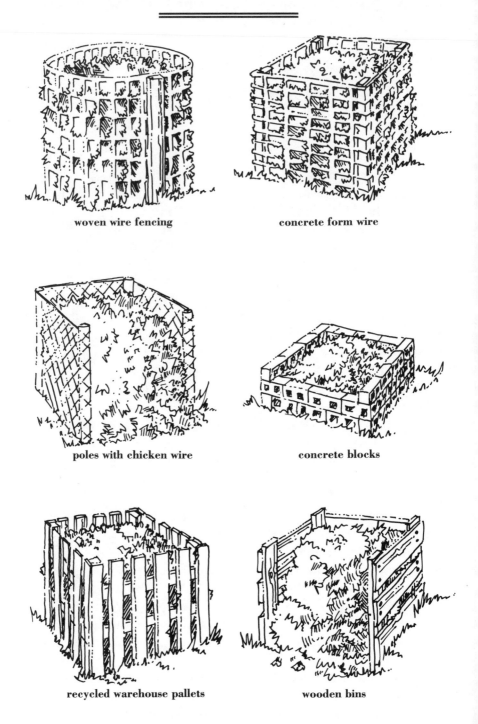

woven wire fencing

concrete form wire

poles with chicken wire

concrete blocks

recycled warehouse pallets

wooden bins

4.6 Composting Containers

Capsicum ciliatum, a wild species unusual for its nonpungency and yellow flowers (rather than the usual white or purple). Note also that the flower is campanulate, or bell-shaped. (Photo by Paul W. Bosland.)

This bird pepper, common to Trinidad, is especially attractive to birds. Seeds for wild varieties such as this may be available through Seed Savers Exchange (see Resources). (Photo by Dave DeWitt.)

Above: The 'NuMex Twilight' is a colorful Ornamental that matures from purple to yellow to orange to red. It is beautiful both as a potted plant and in a formal garden setting. All peppers are edible—even Ornamentals; this one is quite hot. (Photo by Paul W. Bosland.)

Right: Author Dave DeWitt grew these extremely hot wild *chiltepin* from seeds that originated near Douglas, Arizona. (Photo by Dave DeWitt.)

Capsicum baccatum, commonly known as *ají*, a South American pepper with medium heat. They are either yellow or orange in maturity. (Photo by Dave DeWitt.)

Most sources on composting insist that garden soil must be added to the pile to introduce microorganisms. But Dr. Clarence Gouleke, an engineer who researched composting at the University of California at Berkeley, discovered that bacteria and fungal spores occur naturally in the air and on just about any organic material, so adding soil to the pile to "inoculate" it is superfluous. It does not hurt the pile to add soil, but soil does not speed up composting at all and will make the pile bulkier.

Gouleke also discovered that the procedure of shredding all materials into tiny particles is overrated. Shredding does make the pile smaller, but it is not necessary for large, soft materials to be composted such as weed stems or heads of cabbage. Shredding should only be used for large, hard materials such as tree branches, which should not be composted but which can be used as mulch in a flower garden.

Many sources state that the compost pile needs manure in order to add sufficient nitrogen and make the pile heat up. Actually, green matter such as grass clippings will do a good job when applied in a ratio of one part green material to three parts brown (dried) material.

The question of whether or not compost provides enough natural fertilizer is much debated. Some sources insist that compost is actually a soil dressing, not a fertilizer, and that a pint of high-nitrogen fertilizer such as a 12-12-12 (N-P-K) or 10-6-4 should be included each time a layer is added to the pile. They state that the fertilizer not only adds nitrogen, which speeds decomposition, but also adds valuable nutrients missing from the compost.

Organic gardeners disagree and avoid using chemical fertilizers, preferring to add aged manure to the compost pile or directly to the garden. Organic gardeners do concede the point that most compost is low in soluble nitrogen, potassium, and phosphorus. Jack Ruttle observes: "I have grown many fine vegetable gardens with no other fertilizer than an inch or two of pure compost applied once a year, and I have known plenty of other gardeners who do the same." Peppers do not need large amounts of nitrogen, so compost and manure generally provide enough nutrition for the plants.

The Composting Process

Microorganisms decompose the plant material (which is mostly carbon), producing carbon dioxide and heat. As the pile rots, the temperature of the pile may reach 160°F. This heat tends to kill weed seeds and disease organisms, but the cooler parts of the pile will not benefit. Thus, the pile should be turned so that all parts heat up. Another reason for turning the compost is to speed up the decomposition. Each turning cuts the rotting time approximately in half. Unturned piles will be ready in about a year, and the compost will be just as good. How often you turn the pile depends upon how often you need compost in the garden.

Keep the pile covered and protected from rainwater, for the water will leach out potassium and nitrogen. Water the pile with a hose until there is runoff. It should be moist and springy to the touch—like a damp sponge. Then cover the pile with plastic sheeting.

Troubleshooting

Here are common composting problems and their solutions:

STRONG ODOR. The pile is too wet or has insufficient oxygen, so add dry materials or turn the pile.

DAMP BUT NOT PRODUCING HEAT. There is insufficient nitrogen, so add grass clippings or other green matter.

TOO ACIDIC. (This can be found out by measuring the pH with a pH test kit from a gardening store.) Add lime.

DRY AND NOT COMPOSTING. Add water.

TOO HOT, STARTING TO BURN. Turn the pile more often.

SMELLS OF AMMONIA. There is too much nitrogen, so add sawdust, dry leaves, or other high-carbon materials, and turn the pile.

Application

Some gardeners sift the compost from the bins through a one-half-inch mesh screen and return larger particles to the pile for further decomposition. Compost should be applied at the rate of between one and four bushels per hundred square feet of garden and then ro-totilled into the soil. During the growing season a layer two or three inches thick can be used as a mulch if desired. (See chapter 6 for more details on mulching peppers.)

Soil Preparation

Before adding compost, determine your soil type and what steps, other than adding compost, might be necessary to achieve pepper-growing perfection.

The Ideal Soil

It is unlikely that the perfect soil for growing peppers exists in the natural state anywhere in the country, so some soil treatment will undoubtedly be necessary. Generally speaking, the best pepper-growing soil has the following characteristics: a warm, full-sun location; well-drained loam or sandy loam high in organic material but with moderate fertility; a herbicide-free environment; little or no alkali; and a pH registering between 6.0 and 8.0 (ideally between 6.7 and 7.3).

Testing the Soil

Home gardeners commonly apply fertilizers, lime, sulfur, and other materials indiscriminately to their garden plots. Usually, such applications do more harm than good because gardeners believe in the old adage that if one pound is good, two must be better. Gardeners who have any doubts about their soil should have it tested to determine which soil enhancers to apply. Such tests will determine whether a problem in growing healthy plants is due to nutrition or a physical defect in the soil, such as poor texture or chemicals. A glance

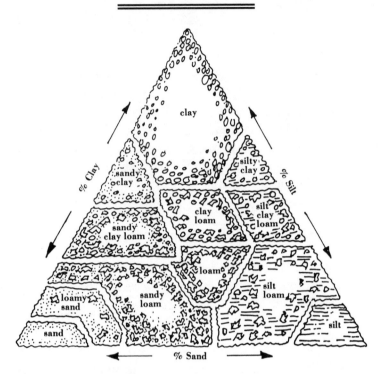

Labels within figure:
clay
% Clay
% Silt
silty clay
sandy clay
clay loam
silt clay loam
sandy clay loam
loam
loamy sand
sandy loam
silt loam
sand
silt
% Sand

4.7   The Soil Triangle, Showing the Percentages of Various Particles

at the soil triangle will give the gardener an idea of how the various soil types relate to one another.

The first step is to contact county extension agents and request information, procedures, and forms for soil testing. In some states, it will be necessary to contact the soil- and water-testing laboratories or agronomy departments of state agricultural universities. Generally speaking, home soil-testing kits are designed for eastern soils and are not accurate for western soils.

Taking soil samples from the garden is a simple procedure. The best method is to take six samples from various parts of the garden and combine them into a composite sample. First, remove any surface litter such as leaves and old stalks. To collect the samples, use either a soil auger or a small shovel and dig down about six to eight inches. Ideally, each sample should measure between six and eight inches long and about one-half to one inch wide. Mix the samples together thoroughly in a clean pail or box. Break up any lumps and allow the composite sample to dry at room temperature. Remove stones and debris and crush the soil so that there are uniform small grains, but do not pulverize it completely. Label the sample, fill out the appropriate form received from the county agent, and mail it.

The soil sample report will typically give the following information: soil type or texture, pH, salinity (expressed as electroconductivity), percentage of organic matter, and fertility status as indicated by the levels of nitrogen, potassium, and phosphorus. Some reports do not include nitrogen content because it is assumed that yearly additions of nitrogen to the garden are necessary. The report will usually make recommendations about what to add to the soil to improve its condition. It will probably not mention drainage, the amount of irrigation needed, or the presence of pesticides or herbicides. In some states, specialized tests also report on zinc, manganese, copper, boron, sulfates, and silt.

Solarizing the Soil

Solarization uses the sun's energy to pasteurize the soil. Temperatures in excess of 125°F will kill soil-borne pests, including pathogens, nematodes, insects, and weed seeds up to four inches below the soil surface, but it takes between four and six weeks of very sunny weather to eliminate disease-causing organisms at greater depths. The soil solarization method has been demonstrated to be very effective for small gardens, and it is a technique commonly used in integrated pest-management systems. The only drawback to solarization is that it should be done in the summer, when air temperatures are high and there is intense solar radiation. Therefore, it is usually applied to fallow plots. In the Southwest, the method will work during the late spring, summer, and early fall.

The soil to be treated should be cleared of plant material, loosened, watered, and covered with a thin, clear, polyethylene film. Use clear film rather than black film because the clear plastic will transmit more solar radiation and increase the temperature of the soil. The thinnest film available (four millimeters) is the least expensive and most effective. The edges of the plastic film should be sealed with a layer of soil to prevent heat loss and to retain moisture.

The soil should be kept damp for the duration of the solarization because more resting fungal spores will be killed in hot, damp soil than in dry soil. Moist soil conducts heat better. A single deep irrigation may be sufficient, but additional moisture will enhance the treatment. A soaker hose may be left under the film if additional watering is needed.

The longer the solarization period, the more organisms will be killed, especially at the greater depths. Solarizing for several weeks is recommended. Remember that solarized soil can become reinfested if contaminated soil is brought into the plot by dirty shoes or tools, so clean all garden shoes and disinfect the rototiller blades, shovels, and hoes with soap and water before using them again.

Solarization also works well for preparing small quantities of garden soil for potted plants. Fill a large, self-closing plastic bag with garden soil and place it in direct sun for several weeks and the soil will become pasteurized.

Correcting Problems

Some steps can be taken to improve the soil for growing peppers and other vegetables.

ACIDIC SOILS. Soils with a low pH can be treated with lime or dolomite to neutralize them. Rates of application for varying degrees of pH are usually listed on the bags of lime.

ALKALINE SOILS. These soils have heavy accumulations of calcium carbonate (lime), which raises the pH to unacceptably high levels. The addition of peat moss, which is slightly acidic, can help neutralize alkaline soils. Organic material also helps improve their workability.

SALINE SOILS. Shallow irrigating and overfertilization cause salts such as sodium bicarbonate, sodium chloride, and magnesium sulfate (which are all present in the irrigation water) to accumulate on the soil as a crust that will burn foliage and kill plants. Usually, saline soils are a problem when the rainfall is insufficient to leach the salts out of the soil. The only remedies for saline soils are good drainage and heavy irrigation to dissolve and remove the salts.

SANDY SOILS. These soils drain quickly and dry out too fast. Compost or other organic material such as aged manure will bind sand particles together, decreasing erosion and assisting in water retention.

CLAY SOILS. Small particles of clay tend to compact and prevent drainage and aeration. The addition of compost, or other organic material such as aged manure, clusters the small clay particles into lumps that will improve drainage and aeration and will make the soil easier to work and more friable (easily crumbled). The addition of about two inches of coarse sand to clay soil will increase drainage. *Never* add sand without adding organic material, or a low-grade cement may form in the garden!

IMPOVERISHED SOILS. The most commonly applied organic nutrients, besides compost, are manures from herbivores such as horses, cattle, goats, poultry, hogs, rabbits, and sheep. Fresh manure is high in ammonia, can burn young plants, and should not be used. Steer manure aged or composted six months to two years provides low to moderate quantities of nitrogen, potassium, and phosphorus and can be applied at the rate of five hundred to one thousand pounds per one thousand square feet of garden. Poultry, rabbit, sheep, and goat manures are higher in nutrients and should be applied at the rate of between two hundred and four hundred pounds per one thousand square feet of garden. For additional information on fertilizing peppers in the garden, see chapter 6.

POOR DRAINAGE. Because one of the most common causes of disease in peppers is fungal infection of the roots caused by poor drainage, it makes sense to have good drainage. Some gardeners, whose soils are high in clay or who live where the water table is high, actually go to the trouble of creating a scree for drainage. Screes are thick layers of crushed rock (or gravel) and sand that are constructed beneath the garden soil and drain water from the plant roots. They are extremely labor intensive to build, however, and raised beds are probably a better solution.

Under extreme conditions, no amount of drainage can prevent disaster. In the summer of 1992, Rick DeWitt's pepper garden in Sarasota, Florida, which was planted in sandy, well-drained soil, was destroyed when seventeen inches of rain fell in just two days. Entire fields of New Mexican chiles in southern New Mexico are wiped out by phytophthora wilt when summer storms dump too much water on already irrigated fields.

CHAPTER 5

Seeds and Seedlings

A pepper garden can only be as good as the original genetic material used to start it—the seed. Bad seed produces unsatisfactory results, no matter how skilled the gardener is. At least good seed stands a chance of producing excellent plants and pods.

Selecting Seed

One of the biggest disappointments for the pepper gardener is to discover that the seed planted does not produce the pods it is supposed to produce. Instead of Jalapeños, say, the gardener finds an unrecognizable hybrid and realizes that time and energy has been wasted by growing this plant. Therefore, it is worthwhile to select good seed.

Home-Grown Seeds

Home gardeners often produce unwanted hybrids (out-crosses) because peppers are notorious cross-pollinators. When different varieties are planted close together in the garden, bees and other insects will carry pollen from flower to flower, cross-pollinating them. The pods of the current year's plants will be true, but the seed in those pods will produce hybrids thereafter.

To produce seed that is true to type, individual varieties must be pollinated only by their own pollen. Commercial seed producers avoid cross-pollination by isolating varieties and planting them at least a mile from one another, which is farther than the average bee flies. Home gardeners can produce true seed by isolating peppers from insects and growing them in greenhouses or under netting. These techniques are described in chapter 8.

Many pepper gardeners exchange seed with other growers, but this seed may also not grow true to type. Home growers can either ask the sender how the seed was grown, or plant it and see what happens. Gardeners and seed collectors from all over the world send us seed, and the more unusual the variety is, the greater our temptation is to grow it regardless of origin.

Commercial Seed

Seed produced by seed companies is generally more reliable than home-grown seed because the companies try to safeguard the genetic purity of the cultivar. They use a systematic seed-growing process, which begins with crop improvement associations in each state. In the association, a plant breeder responsible for developing a specific variety of pepper or other crop produces small quantities of Breeder Seed. That is multiplied into Foundation Seed, which is controlled by the crop improvement association. The association grows the Foundation Seed to produce Registered Seed, which is sold to seed companies to produce Certified Seed for farmers and the general public.

Large seed companies have their own internal process that mirrors the one used by crop improvement associations. Company plant breeders develop Breeder Seed and Foundation Seed for specific varieties. It is then passed on to company seed production managers, who oversee the growing of Registered and Certified Seed. In some cases, the production of Certified Seed is farmed out to independent growers on farms distant from one another to avoid cross-pollination.

Unfortunately, some small seed companies and cottage seed industries either do not practice proper isolation techniques or buy their seed from growers who do not. Thus, their seed is variable and often yields hybrids. Home gardeners should question small seed companies about their isolation techniques, or buy only from the major companies.

Always buy seed from a reliable seed company, one who consistently provides varieties that are true to type, free from disease, and with a high germination percentage. High quality, fresh seed is dependable; cheap seed is neither dependable nor inexpensive.

When buying commercial seed, growers should check the seed packet for a germination percentage. The federal pepper regulations are: Seeds with a germination percentage below 55 percent may not be sold; seeds with a percentage between 55 and 85 percent must have the percentage listed on the packet; seeds with a germination percentage over 85 percent need not have the percentage listed.

Inspecting and Testing Seed

Once the seeds of the selected varieties are in hand, there are several easy culling techniques to increase germination percentage and potential seedling vigor. First, place the seeds in a jar of water and discard any that float. These are damaged, partial seeds and those lacking embryos. Next, inspect the seeds, preferably under a magnifying glass, and remove any that are undersized, shriveled, discolored, cracked, or otherwise damaged.

Some pepper growers, especially those who use direct seeding methods, like to know the expected germination percentage for each variety, so they conduct a germination test in the late winter. Place the seed between damp (not sopping wet) layers of paper towels, with no two seeds touching. Transfer the layers of towels to a plastic bag (preferably a self-closing bag) and set it on something warm, such as heating cables, or on top of the hot water heater or refrigerator. After two weeks have passed, enough time for the average pepper seed to sprout, open the bag and count the sprouted seeds. To arrive at the approximate germination percentage, divide the number of sprouted seeds by the total number of seeds tested. Seed-testing laboratories in every state will conduct this test for a fee, but allow them at least two months to run the test.

Seed Germination

Pepper-seed germination even under optimum conditions is often slow and irregular. Some studies have shown that pepper seeds germinate quickly and have high germination percentages under high temperatures, but some exotic varieties we have grown have taken upwards of five weeks to germinate even at ideal temperatures. Pepper seeds need warmth, oxygen, and moisture to germinate, but, before planting the seed, home gardeners should consider other factors that influence germination.

Pod Maturity, Seed Dormancy, and After-ripening

The maturity of the pods at the time seed is extracted greatly influences germination. Immature pods will usually produce infertile seed, which will not germinate. In 1986, in a study conducted at the Louisiana Agricultural Experiment Station, R. L. Edwards and F. J. Sundstrom extracted seed from red and orange pods of Tabasco peppers harvested 150, 195, and 240 days after transplanting. They tested the seed for germination percentage and found, as expected, that seed from the red pods outperformed seed from the orange pods in all cases. They also discovered that the germination performance of seed from the red pods decreased as the season progressed: the 81 percent germination at 150 days dropped to 63 percent at 240 days. This study indicates that seeds from the earliest picked red pods will have the highest germination percentage, at least for Tabasco peppers.

Some peppers, like other perennials, produce seed that, when extracted from the fresh pods and planted, does not germinate immediately even though all the environmental factors favor germination. This survival mechanism, called dormancy, helps prevent germination in the fall, just before cold weather would kill the seedlings. Because peppers are perennials, but are grown as annuals in the United States, the degree of dormancy varies from variety to variety. The strongest dormancy appears in wild varieties, such as *chiltepins*, which overwinter well. Hybrids grown as annuals have the weakest degree of dormancy.

In the same study, Edwards and Sundstrom also tested the process called after-ripening, which is the gradual drying of the seed so that its moisture content drops from about 34 percent to 7 percent over a three-week period. In one test, the germination percentage of seed from red pods increased from 58 percent to 94 percent after twenty-one days of after-ripening. No significant effect of after-ripening occurred on seed from immature pods.

This study, concurring with our observations over the years, indicates that the highest germination percentage occurs in seed harvested from early red pods that are dried for between one and four months. Some varieties have other colors, such as orange or yellow, at maturity, so growers should pick these pods for seeds when that color reaches its deepest hue. See chapter 8 for information on the collection and storage of seeds.

Temperature and Irrigation

During the winter of 1934–1935, H. L. Cochran of the Georgia Experiment Station conducted a classic study of the effects of temperature and irrigation on the germination of Bell pepper seed. Two flats of seeds were placed in each of five greenhouses, which were kept at the following temperature ranges: 40°F to 50°F, 50°F to 60°F, 60°F to 70°F, 70°F to 80°F, and 90°F to 100°F. In each greenhouse, one of the flats was surface irrigated by a simple watering can, and the other was sub-irrigated by placing it in an inch of water in a large tank until the soil had taken up enough water to dampen the surface.

Both the percentage and speed of germination increased dramatically as the temperature increased. No seeds germinated in the coldest greenhouse. The percentage increased from 59 percent at 50°F to 60°F to 74 percent at 90°F to 100°F. As the temperature rose, the seedlings emerged sooner: they took thirty days to germinate when the temperature was between 50°F and 60°F and six days at 90°F to 100°F. Those seeds that had not germinated even after forty-five days in the coldest greenhouse sprouted in six days when transferred to the hottest greenhouse.

The highest germination percentage (79.5 percent) occurred at 70°F to 80°F, and the quickest germination (six days, 73 percent) occurred at 90°F to 100°F. Watering by subirrigation reduced the germination percentage at all temperatures, probably because that procedure reduced the soil temperature more than surface irrigation did.

The inescapable conclusion from Cochran's experiment, and many subsequent ones, is that for optimum germination, pepper seed should be grown at 70°F or more and should be watered with warm water from the top.

Preplanting Treatments

Cochran also soaked some of the seeds in water before planting, but only for six hours. Soaking the seeds for two or three days can sometimes aid the germination rate and percentage, but probably not significantly.

Some peppers, especially wild varieties such as the *chiltepin*, have a particularly tough seed coat and are slow to germinate. Growers should soak the seeds for five minutes in a 10-percent bleach solution, rinse well, and then plant them. This procedure will soften the seed coat so the seed will germinate more quickly. If the seed has not germinated in fourteen days, the bleach treatment can be repeated.

Gibberellin, a plant hormone, will also increase the germination rate and percentage in peppers. Seed should be soaked for one to two hours in a 100-parts-per-million (ppm) solution. Gibberellin is available from some of the suppliers listed in the Resources.

Peppers are susceptible to plant pathogens, such as bacterial leaf spot and tobacco mosaic virus, on the seed coat. Since the gardener cannot detect such pathogens, a relatively simple preventative procedure has been developed to remove them. First, soak the seeds for one-half hour in a 10-percent (weight to volume) trisodium phosphate (TSP) solution. (TSP is available at most hardware stores as a wall cleaner.) After soaking, rinse the seeds thoroughly in cold running water. Then soak the seeds in a 10-percent bleach solution for five minutes, then rinse them thoroughly in cold running water until all of the bleach odor is gone. Dry the seeds and sow within a month of treatment.

One of the most ingenious preplanting treatments we've come across is the technique developed by Charlie Ward of Virginia Beach, Virginia. Charlie was bothered by the low germination rates of *chiltepin* seeds and then read an article about the spread of *chiltepins* by birds. He decided to prepare a treatment that simulated the alimentary canal of birds. He made a slurry out of seagull excrement, which is plentiful in Virginia Beach, and water, added the seeds, and let the mixture sit in the sun for a few days. After extracting the seeds with forceps and planting them, Charlie discovered that his germination rate increased to 95 percent!

Such a technique can be used by pepper gardeners who also raise birds such as parrots, finches, and canaries. These birds will readily eat small red pods because they contain pro-vitamin A, which improves the color of the birds' plumage. The droppings can be collected on newspaper and the seeds can be removed and planted.

Growing Seedlings

An ideal pepper-growing environment is one that provides optimum levels of light, heat, moisture, and oxygen. The home gardener has a number of options to choose from, but not all of the environments (cold frames, for example) will keep the seeds warm enough for quick, high-percentage germination. We advise that growers use heating cables under their growing containers in all environments. The plastic-covered cables will keep the soil temperature stable, usually between 70°F and 80°F, and are equipped with a thermostat that shuts off the heat when the preset temperature is reached. Carolyn Esparsen, a master gardener, suggests that if cables are not available, the growing containers be placed on top of the refrigerator. Suppliers now offer propagation mats that keep the temperature at 75°F, but they are more expensive than cables.

Greenhouses and Window Greenhouses

Heated greenhouses are probably best for starting seeds indoors. Gardeners fortunate enough to have a greenhouse enjoy plenty of diffused sunlight, heat from solar gain and heaters, humidity from the proximity of other plants, and air circulation from fans. Greenhouses do have a few drawbacks. Some greenhouses, especially those attached to the north side of a house, are not bright enough, and the pepper seedlings become leggy and topple over. In such conditions, the newest growth of the seedlings may need to be pinched back to encourage lateral growth and produce a bushier plant.

Some greenhouses, especially south-facing ones, may overheat during the spring and may need shading. Greenhouse supply stores and some nurseries sell shade cloth of various densities. Greenhouses also need adequate ventilation to avoid damping off and stem rot. (These problems are discussed later.)

Many gardening books suggest that windows are good places to germinate pepper seed and to grow seedlings. This is simply not true. The amount of available light through the windows decreases as the sun rises higher in the sky and the days approach the summer solstice, resulting in spindly plants. Cats are another problem with windowsill cultivation because they are notorious seedling grazers and can quickly ruin a freshly sprouted crop. Cold drafts at night and inadequate air circulation during the day also cause problems.

Window greenhouses, which extend outside the house, are much better than windowsills because they provide more light. They, too, cool down at night, so heating cables should be used under the containers. Unfortunately, window greenhouses lack the space to grow large numbers of seedlings and they tend to trap hot air, so they must be well ventilated. If used carefully, they are fine for the gardener who is raising only a few favorite peppers.

Cold Frames and Hotbeds

Cold frames are the second most efficient environment for growing seedlings and probably the least expensive to construct and operate. There are two types of cold frames: permanent ones, and temporary ones that are dismantled after the seedlings are transplanted.

A cold frame is a wooden box with a glass, plastic, or fiberglass

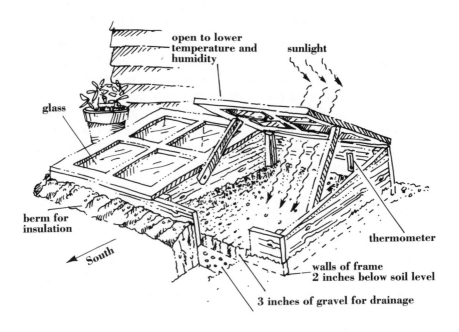

5.1   A Cold Frame

top. Permanent cold frames can be constructed in various sizes; those about three feet wide and six feet long are average. Gardeners should take into consideration the dimensions of the growing containers. For instance, the average tray for six-pack cells measures eleven by twenty-one inches, so the cold frame should be constructed to accommodate multiples of those measurements.

The top of the cold frame can be made of old window sashes, or a wooden frame covered with fiberglass or plastic film. Some greenhouse supply stores sell portable cold frames or premade sashes for cold frames. The top should be hinged so that it can be propped open during the day for ventilation. The cold frame should face south so that the top is angled to catch the rays of the sun. It should be equipped with a thermometer and heating cables and should be sealed with weather stripping or caulking. Permanent cold frames should have good drainage and installed heating cables covered with wire screening and sand to insure even heating.

Temporary cold frames can be constructed of cinderblocks sealed with plastic film, or from old lumber that can be knocked apart and stored after use. Both permanent and temporary cold frames can be insulated by mounding a berm of soil or sawdust around the frame. Electric light bulbs can be installed in cold frames for additional heating. During a typical spring day, the cold frame should be opened when the sun's first rays strike it in the morning and closed in the late afternoon to retain the heat inside. (Hotbeds are simply cold frames with heating cables installed. They are doubly useful because the temperature can be raised so that seed germinates quickly and the seedlings grow well. Then the heat can be turned off so that the seedlings can harden off, a procedure discussed below.)

Some growers have their cold frames perform double duty in the winter as composting sites. Commonly composted materials such as kitchen vegetable scraps, rabbit manure, and other organic material is placed in the cold frame. Despite the cold outside temperatures, the solar gain in the cold frame causes the material to compost over the winter months, and it's ready for spring planting.

Artificial Light

Some gardeners do not even have an outdoor garden. They prefer to raise their peppers from seedlings to fruiting plants in

5.2   A Fluorescent Light Stand for Seedlings

containers under artificial light. (See chapter 8 for a complete discussion of this technique.) Outdoor gardeners without either a greenhouse or cold frame can successfully germinate seeds and grow seedlings under fluorescent lights.

All that's needed are one or two four-foot-long fluorescent fixtures mounted on a stand or hung from the rod in a spare closet. Garden mail-order companies and retail shops sell a number of models of light stands on wheels. Any cool-white fluorescent bulb will work. The containers are placed beneath the lights so that, when the seedlings germinate, they are only a few inches from the bulbs. The fluorescent bulbs will warm the containers, but will not burn the tender foliage. The inverse square law applies here: doubling the distance between the bulbs and the plants results in only one-quarter of the amount of light reaching the foliage. Bulbs placed too far from the seedlings will cause spindly plants.

Seedlings should grow well under artificial light, but they may become leggy and need to be pinched back. Also, they are tempting targets for cats or pet birds to munch on. These seedlings will be more tender than those grown in a greenhouse or cold frame, and may need a more careful process of hardening off, as they will be more susceptible to sunburn and wind damage.

Containers

When choosing containers consider the number of seedlings for each variety of pepper that will be sprouted, the size of the seedlings when they are transplanted, and whether a one-step or two-step method will be used. In a one-step method, seedlings are usually raised in a peat pot or a cube of biodegradable material that will disintegrate in the garden. In a two-step method, the seedlings grow in six-pack cells until they have reached the four- to five-leaf stage, are then transplanted into larger pots, and from there are set in the garden.

Home gardeners who only grow about two plants each of about five varieties will not have space problems, so they might as well plant seeds in six-inch or larger plastic pots or peat pots and thin them to one plant per pot. Six-pack cells in plastic trays are by far the easiest and most space-effective containers to use when growing large quantities of many varieties of peppers.

One drawback of the cell packs is that the roots of the seedlings sometimes become cramped and start circling the inside of each cell. Root cramping sets back the seedling if the roots are not gently untangled. A root continues to grow in the direction in which it is set in the ground, so one that is not pointed outward will not grow out. Two more drawbacks should be noted. Root-bound plants tend to dry out and need water more often, and sometimes vigorously growing seedlings compete for sunlight as they bush out. The obvious solution here is to transplant cramped seedlings into larger containers.

Commercial nurseries use a slightly different two-step process: The seeds are germinated in open flats and the tender, two-leafed seedlings are transplanted into the cell packs after a couple of days. This method insures that cells are not wasted on nongerminating seeds.

5.3   Germination Containers

Growing Media

The perfect medium for germinating and growing seedlings has good drainage and aeration, but retains some moisture. The medium should promote rapid root expansion, which produces a vigorous growth of foliage. The particles should be fairly large so that the medium does not pack together but allows the roots easy penetration. Dense or clay soils are the worst possible media for growing seedlings because the roots are drowned in water and receive no oxygen.

Every pepper gardener has their own preference for the soil mixture for raising seedlings. Soil mixtures may range from commercial potting mixtures to garden soil to various blends of organic and inorganic materials. Some companies sell propagation systems that combine the elements of a cover, an insulated growing tray, capillary matting, and a water reservoir. The key is to find the best environment for the seedlings. For example, the combination of a peat pot and a loose mix might work well in humid areas, but could dry out too quickly in arid environments.

Although some growers believe that peppers should be germinated in the soil in which they will eventually live, we do not recommend using garden soil. It is usually too dense for the tender plants and may contain disease-causing organisms. Gardeners who insist on using garden soil should sterilize it by baking it for at least an hour in the oven at 350°F. Then it should be mixed half and half with soil expanders such as as perlite or vermiculite.

Various commercial media are on the market, notably Jiffy Mix and Pro-Mix, which are usually combinations of milled peat moss or sphagnum moss, fine vermiculite, and fertilizer. These pasteurized mixtures work well in most situations, but sometimes are unavailable to the home gardener. You can prepare a custom seedling medium by mixing together readily available materials that meet the criteria for drainage, moisture retention, and aeration. We use commercial, sterile potting soil, perlite, and vermiculite mixed in equal proportions. Coarse sand can be substituted for the perlite, but never use builder's sand (too fine) or ocean beach sand (too salty). Peat moss is difficult to wet, is too acid, and compacts badly, so use it sparingly. Potting soil and vermiculite hold moisture and nutrients, and the perlite prevents compaction, aids in drainage and aeration, and promotes root growth.

Propagating Seedlings

To grow seedlings for transplanting we use the following technique with excellent results. Although we use it in semiarid New Mexico, it should work equally well in other parts of the country. We use greenhouses for our growing environment.

About six to eight weeks before transplanting, prepare six-pack cells by filling them with the suggested growing medium, and place the cells in the plastic trays. Place the trays on the heating cables and plug in the cables. Because the medium has virtually no nutrients, water the cells with a diluted solution of a 20-20-20 fertilizer (one-half teaspoon in one gallon of water) or a slow-release fertilizer, such as 10-10-10.

Select the seeds according to the criteria described earlier and use a preplanting treatment if you wish. With a stick or the eraser end of a pencil, punch a hole in each cell one-fourth inch deep. Drop two or three seeds in each hole, then cover them with the planting medium. In each six-pack, insert a plastic tag with the variety name and the date marked on it in permanent ink or pencil. Some growers keep a journal in which they record the variety name, date, number of seeds planted, and later, the germination percentage and other notes on the progress of their seeds.

When the seeds sprout, cull all but the most vigorous seedlings from each cell by clipping them at the base with scissors. Gently water the plants from the top and make certain the cells are kept moist, but do not allow water to sit in the trays and keep the mixture soggy. If the seedlings are stressed at all by drying out or wilting, it will be difficult if not impossible to revive their normal growth. Make certain there is adequate ventilation and air circulation in the growing environment. Fertilize the cell packs once a week with the mixture described above.

In a heated greenhouse, the heating cables can be turned off after the seeds have sprouted. In a cold frame where the only heat is from cables, the cables should be kept on until the nighttime temperatures warm above freezing.

Cigarette smokers should wash their hands with a strong soap or with rubbing alcohol before touching the seeds or seedlings. The tobacco in cigarettes may contain tobacco mosaic virus, which can infect the pepper seeds or plants.

Pests and Disease

The same friendly environment that promotes seedling growth also provides perfect breeding conditions for common greenhouse pests such as aphids, whiteflies, mealybugs, and spider mites. Aphids are probably the most common. Although spraying with dilute nicotine sulfate or Diazinon solutions will kill them, it is not the best solution because the chemicals can burn the leaves and stems of the seedling, inhibiting its growth. A nontoxic method is to wash the aphids off the seedlings every day with a stream of water. This procedure is labor intensive, but it works. Another method is to spray the seedlings with a diluted solution of Ivory soap or insecticidal soap.

Mealybugs are soft-bodied insects that look like pieces of white fluff. They do not move around much, but once they are established they can suck plenty of sap out of pepper plants. The least toxic way to kill them is to touch them with a swab dipped in isopropyl alcohol.

Whiteflies, another common greenhouse pest, are more difficult to kill because they are so mobile. They can be controlled, but probably not eliminated, by closing up the greenhouse and fumigating it by spraying a flying insect insecticide. The greenhouse should stay closed up for ten minutes and then ventilated. Also useful are the yellow, sticky cards that attract the flies and trap them.

By far the most difficult pests to control are spider mites, barely visible eight-legged arachnids that build small webs on the underside of leaves and thus are hard to spot. They can be controlled by spraying the underside of pepper leaves with insecticidal soap or Diazinon, according to the manufacturer's instructions. We always prefer the mechanical removal of pests by water spraying or gentle scraping rather than by the application of chemical insecticides.

The most devastating problem in the humid greenhouse is damping-off, a fungal disease that causes the stem base to rot and the seedling to topple over. Damping-off can quickly wipe out an entire greenhouse of seedlings. The disease proliferates in still, very moist air, so the first line of defense is good air circulation. In humid growing environments, an extra fan to blow air around is a necessity. The seedlings also can be treated with the fungicide Benomyl, according to the manufacturer's instructions.

Hardening-Off

In the protected environment of a greenhouse, cold frame, or indoors under lights, seedlings tend to grow rapidly and produce large cells with thin walls. This soft growth, as it's called, has not prepared the seedling for the rigors of the early spring garden. Its leaves are not accustomed to the strong ultraviolet rays of the sun, its stems are not strong enough to withstand high winds, its roots are not established enough for dry conditions, and the entire plant is subject to shock at low temperatures. Unless properly conditioned for the outside, pepper seedlings may be sunburned, windwhipped, and injured by low temperatures or even heavy rains.

The solution is a process called hardening-off, whereby the seedlings are gradually made tough enough for the garden. Technically, hardening-off is a physiological process that adds carbohydrate reserves to the plant and produces additional cuticle on the leaves, reducing water loss. Practically, the process slows plant growth while acclimating the seedling to harsher conditions.

A cold frame works the best for the hardening-off process. The heating cables are turned off and the top is left open for increasingly longer periods of time (all night when the temperatures are warm enough), so that the seedlings toughen up in the sun, wind, and lower temperatures.

Greenhouse-grown plants, or those grown indoors under lights, are usually taken outside for increasingly long periods of time. Starting about two weeks before transplanting or about the date of the average last frost, move the trays into partial sun. Bring them indoors at night, but turn the greenhouse heaters off. Begin with only a few hours a day outside. As the days go by, increase the amount of sun the seedlings receive and the length of time outdoors until they can be left out all day and night. Reducing the water to older seedlings will also "harden" the plants. Allow the seedlings to wilt slightly before watering them. After two weeks of this treatment they can be transplanted.

Transplanting

By now, the gardener will have already planned the basic design of the garden according to the criteria described in chapter 4. The next decision is where to place the peppers within this design, especially if other crops are being grown. The first consideration is voiced by John Swan, a pepper grower in West Chester, Pennsylvania: "We don't plant peppers in the same location two years in a row; a plot plan reminds us of what we have planted, when and where, from year to year." Crop rotation is crucial for commercial growers; it is merely advisable for home gardeners. If compost is added to the garden each year, and there is no sign of disease, peppers can sometimes be grown for years in the same locations in the garden.

Many gardening authorities, especially those who favor all-organic techniques, instruct the grower to plant peppers with other "companion plants" that are supposedly compatible with them. One book lists basil, carrots, eggplant, onions, parsley, and tomatoes as companion plants for peppers and kohlrabi as an incompatible plant. Unfortunately, such claims must be relegated to the domain of gardening lore; there is no scientific evidence to support them. In some cases, so-called companion plants for peppers, such as tomatoes and eggplants, are closely related and share many of the same diseases and insect pests. Because one may infect another, they can hardly be called good companions.

More reasonable is the concept of intercropping, by which gardeners take into consideration such factors as how fast the various crops mature, their relative heights, and the positioning of light-demanding and shade-tolerant plants. For example, a row of shade-tolerant *rocoto* chile peppers or *chiltepins* might be planted between two rows of corn.

For cultivating large numbers of peppers, the simplest method is to plant them in elevated rows or in clusters in raised beds. Whatever method is used, remember to label each variety or draw a diagram to remind you where it is. It is frustrating to lose track of a certain variety, especially in the early stages before the pods have matured.

Buying Transplants

Of course, we recommend that gardeners raise their own transplants from seed, but some people will be tempted by the healthy-looking seedlings available from commercial nurseries. The main drawback of nursery-grown transplants is the lack of variety available—usually you will find only some Bells and perhaps Jalapeños and Yellow Wax peppers. Also a problem is that some transplants are "forced" with high levels of nitrogen, resulting in tall plants with insufficient root growth. These plants may wilt severely when transplanted.

The opposite problem is one of too many roots, because the seedlings have been growing in cramped containers for too long. It takes longer for pot-bound seedlings to extend their roots into the garden soil, so they, too, are subject to wilting until they are established.

Most nurseries indicate that their seedlings are hardened-off and are ready for immediate transplanting. Instead of taking a chance and being disappointed, harden them off yourself for at least a week.

Technique

The ideal weather for transplanting is marked by cool temperatures, cloudy skies, and little or no wind. After deciding the layout of the peppers, use a trowel to dig a small hole slightly larger than the root ball of the seedling. Holding it by the root ball (never by the stem or leaves if it can be avoided), place the seedling in the hole, fill the rest of the hole with garden soil, press the soil around the root ball and stem, and immediately water it.

Plant spacing depends on a number of factors, including the ultimate size of the varieties being grown. Smaller varieties, such as Ornamentals, can be planted closer together than, say, *ajís*, which grow quite large. Arthur Pratt, a professor emeritus at Cornell University, suggests close spacing for peppers, placing them on one-foot centers. "I do know that pepper plants grow almost twice as tall when they're tightly spaced," he told *Organic Gardening*, "and then there's usually less sunscald on the fruit because they're better shaded by the leaves." Some commercial pepper growers, among them Jeff Campbell of

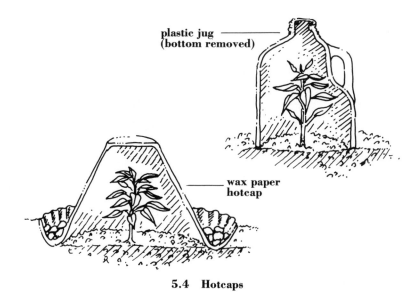

plastic jug
(bottom removed)

wax paper
hotcap

5.4 Hotcaps

Stonewall, Texas, space their plants as closely as four inches apart. Close spacing also helps to keep moisture under the canopy of leaves.

Hotcaps

To protect the seedlings from insects, wind, and cold temperatures, some gardeners set miniature greenhouses, known as hotcaps, over each seedling. Hotcaps, in the form of waxed paper cones, can be purchased at garden stores. They can also be fashioned from glass or plastic jugs. The bottoms of the jugs are cut off, and the remainder of the jug is set over the plant and pushed into the soil. The only problem with hotcaps is that on warm, sunny days they can hold so much heat they can cook the seedlings. They must then be removed during the day and replaced in the early evening.

John and Ann Swan, pepper growers in West Chester, Pennsylvania, cut the bottoms out of six-inch plastic nursery pots and place one around each pepper seedling. "They shelter young seedlings not only from cutworms, but also from stem-whipping winds. The pots reflect and concentrate heat, and give us a reservoir for watering." The Swans also cover their plants with three-gallon plastic nursery pots if night temperatures fall too low.

Direct Seeding

Among the most common weeds in the pepper garden are volunteer peppers from the previous year's fallen pods, which proves that direct seeding works. The technique is mostly used by commercial growers who have acres of pepper plants and don't want to bother with raising transplants.

Direct seeding can be used by the home gardener. The technique is not, however, recommended for climates with short growing seasons. The seed should be planted no more than one-half inch below the soil surface, and the row or grouping of peppers should be carefully marked to identify the variety.

CHAPTER 6

The Growing Season

After being transplanted, peppers seem to sit and do nothing for a few weeks. Although they may not seem to be growing very fast, they are putting out roots and preparing for an enormous surge of growth. Sometimes there will be leaf damage from the sun and wind until the plants adapt to being in the ground.

The Advantages of Mulching

Mulch is any material applied over the surface of the soil to retard the growth of weeds, conserve moisture in the soil, maintain a uniform soil temperature, and improve the appearance of the garden. There is no doubt that mulches increase the yield of pepper plants. Experiments in Canada by Stephen Monette and K. A. Stewart showed that black plastic mulch increased the yields of Bell peppers, which produced more fruit per plant; the pods themselves did not weigh more. Interestingly enough, they also discovered that the yield of pepper plants protected by a windbreak increased, but only when the peppers were not mulched.

A wide variety of mulches has been used with peppers, and determining the one that is right for the home garden depends upon a number of factors including climate and decomposition rates of the mulch. Gardeners should remember that, because mulching warm soils keeps them warm and mulching cold soils tends to keep them cold, the mulch should be applied after the soil warms.

Organic Materials

Lawn clippings, leaves, straw, compost, bark, wood chips, and pine needles have all been used for mulching peppers. These mulches do not affect the soil temperature very much, but they do control weeds and maintain moisture in the soil. They should be used only in regions wet enough to allow them to decompose into the soil. Otherwise, those materials that decay slowly, such as wood or bark chips, will have to be raked out of the plot each year before the soil is roto-tilled. Some growers believe that grass clippings are particularly helpful because thick layers of them can be thoroughly saturated to increase the humidity around pepper leaves and flowers in dry weather. This practice sometimes promotes disease.

Clear Plastic

A clear plastic mulch warms the soil by about 10°F or 12°F but does not control weeds. It should not be used in hot climates. It is not biodegradable and must be removed at the end of the growing season.

Black Plastic

Excellent for controlling weeds, black plastic also warms the soil (up to 5°F) and is good for moisture control. It, too, should not be used in hot climates because it may overheat the plants. Black plastic does not decompose and must be removed at the end of the growing season. There are, however, some brands of black plastic that do decompose.

Researchers at the University of New Hampshire have developed a black plastic mulch with the heat-transmitting qualities of clear plastic. It's called IRT (Infra-Red Transmitting) Mulch and is available from mail-order companies and garden shops.

Foils and Colored Plastic

L. L. Black, a researcher in Louisiana, discovered that aluminum foil produced higher yields of Bell peppers than ordinary black plastic did. Reflective mulches also drastically reduced aphid infestations in peppers, thus lowering the incidents of aphid-transmitted viruses, such as tobacco etch. Black's findings showed that plants mulched with aluminum foil yielded 58 percent more than those mulched with black plastic and 85 percent more than unmulched peppers.

Further experiments by Wayne Porter and William Etzel at Louisiana State University confirmed that aluminum-colored plastic works very well: "The increased yields were probably due to increased light reflection of the aluminum-painted polyethylene." Some gardeners manage to increase the available light by laying aluminum foil between their rows of peppers. This practice should only be followed in humid climates. In the Southwest, for example, with its dry air and high levels of ultraviolet light, the plants would bake.

Robert Dufault and Samuel Wiggins of the University of Vermont's Horticultural Research Center experimented with white plastic mulches on Bell peppers and discovered that the yield of white-mulched peppers was 35 percent greater than those left unmulched.

Michael Kasperbauer and Patrick Hunt of the USDA's Coastal Plains Research Center in Florence, South Carolina, experimented with the effects of black, white, red, and yellow mulches on Bell peppers. The plants grown with the red mulch were taller and heavier than those grown on the other plastics. Their theory is that the phytochrome protein in peppers and other plants is a biological light sensor that responds to red light, particularly far-red, which is beyond the range of human vision. Plant leaves reflect far-red light so, when a mulch reflects far-red, the plant reacts as if competing plants are nearby and puts out more leaves and grows taller.

Some mail-order companies and garden shops are selling three-layer weed mats that prevent weeds but let air, water, and nutrients through.

Newspaper and Other Paper

A favorite mulch that works especially well in the Southwest is ordinary newspaper. Although the sheets must be weighted down with soil to prevent them from blowing away, the newspaper retards weeds, reflects more light than black plastic does, holds moisture in the soil, and can simply be rototilled into the soil at the end of the growing season. Use a thickness of at least two sheets after the transplants have been set out. Avoid using colored newsprint because it takes longer to decompose.

6.1   Newspaper Mulch in a Southwestern Garden

Some gardeners prefer brown paper from shopping bags, cardboard (which works best in a flat garden), or black, biodegradable paper mulch made from peat moss and recycled cardboard, which can also be rototilled. The latter works well in cold climates.

Irrigation Techniques

Simple experiments have revealed that doubling the water applied to peppers doubles their yield—to a point. If the ground becomes too saturated, the water may either suffocate the roots or promote fungal diseases. Adequate watering increases yields and makes the peppers taste better.

Some pepper gardeners are fortunate to live in areas where the only water needed for the garden comes from rainfall. But most gardeners will have to irrigate their moisture-demanding peppers. Gardeners should adjust the frequency and amount of watering to rainfall cycles. In other words, do not irrigate if there has just been a heavy downpour. Rainfall can be deceptive because sometimes it wets the mulch thoroughly but does not penetrate to the deeper roots of pepper plants—some of which are two feet below the surface. Also remember that peppers grown next to large, water-demanding plants, such as corn, may need extra water.

In 1992 we learned an important lesson about watering in our home garden. One of the New Mexican varieties wilted and died,

A family stand selling pepper *ristras* and wreaths at the Labor Day chile festival in Hatch, New Mexico. The festival features a chili-cooking contest and arts and crafts. (Photo by Paul W. Bosland.)

Serranos—one of the most popular chile peppers in Mexico and the Southwest—are cut up
and used fresh in salsas. (Photo by Dave DeWitt.)

An ornamental Piquin, which matures from a dark purple to red and has very hot fruit. The purple stage is so dark, some call these "black" peppers. (Photo by Paul W. Bosland.)

An immature 'Hungarian Paprika'. (*Paprika* means "pepper" in Hungarian.) These are used in Hungary as a vegetable while still yellow; when they mature to red, they are dried and crushed into a powder. They can be hot, spicy, or mild, depending on the variety. (Photo by Paul W. Bosland.)

apparently from phytophthora, but none of the other thirty plants in the garden showed any wilt symptoms. We assumed we were over-watering and restricted the water. The result? Three other plants were stressed from underwatering and nearly died. So the fact that a single plant wilted misled us into a false assumption, and the simple fact remains that occasionally a plant will die from a disease that is not prevalent in the entire plot.

Sprinklers

Overhead sprinkling works fine when the plants in the garden are small. But once they gain some height, the water from the sprinkler is blocked and the garden is not watered evenly. Because it is awkward to keep raising the sprinkler above the foliage, at this point another watering method should be used.

Flood Irrigation

Simply flooding the garden with water from a hose will work well if the drainage is good and is recommended for ridges and furrows, flat beds, and modified irrigated beds (see chapter 4). Carefully watch the time it takes the water to drain from the plot and adjust the amount of water applied to avoid overirrigating. After the hose is turned off, the water should drain from the garden in less than an hour. If it takes any longer, too much water has been applied. Use less water more frequently.

Drip Irrigation

Also called trickle irrigation, this method uses small plastic tubes to apply small but steady amounts of water slowly to each plant in the garden. The main advantages of drip irrigation are that it conserves water because less is lost to evaporation, and it delivers water efficiently to individual plants. There are disadvantages. It is expensive, and the tubes, valves, and other components are likely to break, clog up, get cut with shovels or hoes, and generally fall apart. The drip system must be constantly checked to make sure it is delivering water; otherwise, the gardener risks severe drying of plants. George Brookbank, a master gardener, advises: "Use a drip irrigation system like

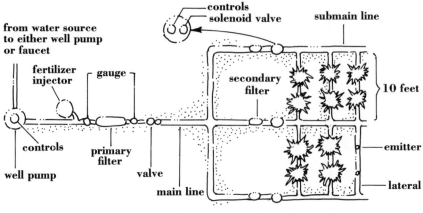

6.2   A Drip Irrigation System

you would any other irrigation system—don't expect too much
from it."

Studies of trickle-irrigated chile peppers in New Mexico indicated that it is the quantity of water applied that increases yield—not
the method of applying the water. Gardeners using drip irrigation
should take care that the soil around peppers remains moist but
not wet. They should also have a backup system in case the drip
system fails.

Fertilizing

There is a great divergence of opinion about fertilizing pepper plants.
D. J. Cotter of New Mexico State University made a succinct observation: "The chile plant appears to be relatively insensitive to soil-
applied nutrients." He has cited studies of New Mexican varieties that
indicated little or no yield increases when nitrogen was applied during
the growing season. He also wrote, "Chile appears to be non-
responsive to phosphorus."

Cotter was referring to the effect of fertilizers on fruit yield.
Pepper *plants* respond very well to fertilizers, but that response is
mostly vegetative. Jeff Campbell, who grows peppers in Stonewall,
Texas, told us the story of his attempt to fertilize Tabasco plants with
large quantities of worm casings. The casings were so loaded with ni-

trogen that his plants grew six feet tall, and not one of them had a single pod!

Excessive nitrogen causes the plant to return to vegetative growth and abort flowers and small pods. Seedlings can be fertilized with fairly high levels of nitrogen to encourage strong vegetative growth, but after the plants have adjusted to the garden, fertilizers need not be applied unless the plants show symptoms of a nitrogen deficiency, such as leaf yellowing and stunted growth. Then they should be fertilized modestly. A lack of nitrogen can cause poor foliage growth, which exposes pods to direct sunlight and causes sunscald.

Most home pepper gardeners will be able to raise great pepper crops simply by adding compost and aged manure to the garden each year. Nearly all commercial growers fertilize before planting and apply fertilizer regularly throughout the growing season, undoubtedly because the heavy concentration of peppers depletes the soil and because manure and compost are not generally added to commercial fields. The fertilization practices of commercial growers are detailed in chapter 10.

Fighting the Weeds

Peppers do not compete well with weeds. More than 150 types of weeds harbor insect-transmitted viruses that can harm peppers. Weeds often grow faster than peppers grow and can cut off sunlight, while stealing nutrients and moisture from the soil. They are also unsightly and produce seeds that will sprout in the garden the following year.

If the garden is mulched properly, weeds will not be a big problem, but vigilance is always necessary in a pepper garden. Some species of weeds grow right next to the pepper stem and will be difficult to see under the canopy of leaves. Some weeds, such as Bermuda grass and bindweed, can invade the garden from other parts of the yard, cross over the top of the mulch, and sometimes establish themselves next to pepper plants.

Gardeners should take pride in their pepper patch and remove weeds by hand, because hoes and shovels can damage leaves, stems, and the roots of peppers grown on ridges. Herbicides need not ever be used in the home garden, although some commercial growers need them (see chapter 10).

Flowering

Flowers begin to form when the pepper plant branches. Flowering is dicotamous, meaning that one flower forms, then two, then four, then eight, and so on. The number of flowers produced is very large compared to those that actually set fruit, and a larger percentage of the early flowers set fruit than the later flowers. The key factor affecting fruit-set is night temperature, which ideally should be between 65°F and 80°F. Fruit will not set when the temperature is above 86°F at night because of excessive transpiration, which causes the blossoms to drop. Blossoms also drop because of excessive nitrogen, high winds, and lack of pollination. If daytime temperatures exceed 95°F, pollen will abort and the fruit-set will be reduced.

In some cases, spraying hormones, such as Bloom Set, on the flowers may prevent blossom drop. A home remedy calls for spraying the blossoms with a solution of one teaspoon of Epsom salts in one quart of water. According to lore, the magnesium in the Epsom salts assists in the setting of fruit.

Pollination

Peppers are usually considered to be a self-pollinated crop. Pepper plants do self-pollinate, but their ability to cross-pollinate is far greater than expected. As early as 1892, J. H. Hart, the superintendent of the Royal Botanical Gardens in Trinidad, reported: "We do not make any specific distinction between the *Capsicums* from here for the simple reason that they degenerate so quickly to a simple form under cultivation that we cannot refer to them as more than a single species. Some of the finest will in four or five generations be nothing more than 'bird-pepper' of which the forms are as many as the days of the year." Hart, of course, was allowing his peppers to cross-pollinate and later planting the seeds of natural hybrids, thus obliterating distinct varieties.

In 1938, M. L. Odland and A. M. Porter of the University of Connecticut suspected that, because of fruit variability, there was a higher percentage of natural cross-pollination in peppers than in to-matoes. Their classic study of the crosses (produced by growing different varieties next to one another) revealed cross-pollination rates averaging 16.5 percent, with a high of 36.8 percent in an Ornamental variety. They noted that "the pepper flower is rather inconspicuous and non-fragrant, a fact that would suggest insect pollination not very likely." But upon close examination of their test plots, they concluded that honey bees were responsible for the cross-pollination, and that "the wind accounts for only a very small percent, if any, of the cross-pollination that takes place in this crop."

An examination of the flowers of wild species, and wild types of the *annuum* species, reveals large drops of nectar. These drops reward bees for visiting the flowers.

In 1984, Steven Tanksley of New Mexico State University found that the rate of natural cross-pollination in New Mexican varieties was far higher that suspected—up to 42 percent cross-pollination. Bees were the culprits again—sweat bees, honey bees, bumblebees, and leaf-cutter bees. His findings demonstrated the need for strict isolation in the production of commercial seed. Other insects known to transmit pollen are ants, aphids, and butterflies.

Any two varieties of the same pod type or species will cross; Jalapeños, for instance, will cross with Piquins. Within the *annuums*, all varieties of all pod types will cross.

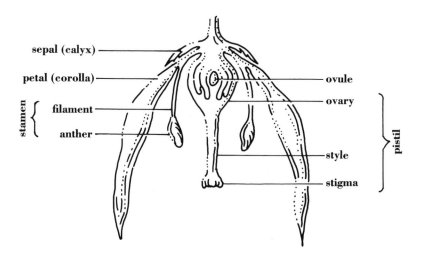

6.3   Cross Section of a Pepper Flower

annuum: Crosses prolifically with *chinense*, sporadically with *baccatum* and *frutescens*, and not at all with *pubescens*

baccatum: Crosses sporadically with *annuum*, *chinense*, and *frutescens*, producing only sterile hybrids; does not cross with *pubescens*

chinense: Crosses prolifically with *annuum*, sporadically with *frutescens* and *baccatum*, and not at all with *pubescens*

frutescens: Crosses sporadically with *annuum*, *baccatum*, and *chinense*; does not cross with *pubescens*

pubescens: Does not cross with any of the other species

Gardeners can now determine which peppers will cross and which will not. For example, nothing will cross with a *rocoto*, so all *rocoto* seeds produced in a mixed garden will be true. It is somewhat safe to plant *ajís* next to Habaneros, because they only sporadically cross. Likewise it is somewhat safe to plant Tabascos next to Jalapeños or Habaneros. It is relatively easy to produce hybrids of the *annuum* varieties with Habaneros. In some cases, the viability of the first-generation seed depends on which species pollinates the other. When *frutescens* pollinates *annuum*, there is no viable seed, but when *annuum* pollinates *frutescens*, there is a limited amount of viable seed.

Fruiting

Fruit development is enhanced by increased sunlight. The size and shape of the pod is inherited, but is subject to considerable modification by the environment. The size of the pods on the same plant tends to decrease slightly as the growing season progresses. Generally speaking, fruits are ready for picking in their fresh green stage at about seventy days after planting. Fully mature pods may take one hundred thirty days or more for some varieties.

Fruit Load

The maximum weight of fruits that a fruiting plant can bear is known as its fruit load. The fruit load of each pepper plant depends on a number of considerations including stem size, amount of

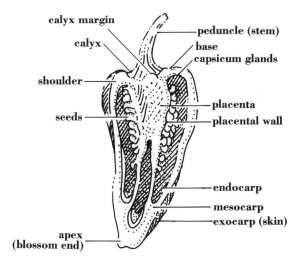

6.4   Cross Section of a Pepper Pod

foliage, and the extent of the root system. When the plant achieves its fruit load, it ceases flowering. Thus a plant will stop producing fruit even though there may be a month or more left in the growing season.

The pepper gardener can increase the yield of plants by picking pods in their largest immature green form. The plant, not having to bear the weight of those pods, will continue flowering and setting fruit throughout the remainder of the season, and the total weight of pods produced by each plant will be greater.

The technique of periodic harvesting to increase pod yields only works in long growing seasons or with varieties with very short growing periods. In cooler climates, pepper plants may not reach their fruit load before the first killing frost, so picking pods early will not increase the total yield.

Pungency

Mature pods are more pungent than immature pods. Stressing pepper plants usually increases their pungency. The restriction of water, or overwatering, will increase the amount of capsaicinoids in the pods. Pungency is also increased when the fruit ripens at higher temperatures rather than cooler ones. In fact, the pods of New Mexican varieties ripening at temperatures between 86°F and 95°F have twice as many capsaicinoids as those ripening at 59°F to 72°F. Nitrogen that is applied after fruit-set can lower the capsaicinoid levels.

Pepper lore holds that the seeds are the hottest part of the pod, but this is not true. Although the seeds do absorb capsaicinoids during processing, such as drying or roasting and peeling, in the fresh pods they are not very pungent at all. The most pungent part of the pod is the placental tissue, or cross wall, which holds the seeds and produces the capsaicinoids. The pepper pod becomes less pungent from the stem end to the apex.

Flavor

Each variety of pepper has a set of aromatic substances that give it a unique flavor. The important flavor component of Bells and Jalapeños is 2-isobutyl-3-methoxyprazine. This chemical is the most potent aroma known to humankind and is detectable when diluted to one drop in an Olympic-sized swimming pool full of water. The Tabasco has twenty-three flavor components rather than a single dominant compound. The Habanero has a particular, fruity aroma that is never forgotten. Gardeners should pick fresh pods, cut them open, and smell and taste them to decide which are better for various culinary applications.

Improving the Yield

In addition to the methods described above, pepper gardeners have discovered other ways to produce more pods. One of the most common practices is the removal of flowers and early fruit. Dr. William Clapham, a plant physiologist at the University of Maine, recommends pinching off flowers for several weeks to increase the dry weight of the fruit. He suggests that the pepper plants devote their energy to vegetative growth rather than fruit production, resulting in larger plants that produce more market-sized fruits. In another experiment, plants from which all the flowers had been removed as late as mid-July still had good yields.

Howard Watson of Houston, Texas, grows his Bell peppers in plastic-wrapped cages. He makes wire cages eighteen to twenty inches in diameter and about five feet high, and then wraps the bottom half of the cage with six-millimeter clear polyethylene. In the garden each cage encloses a single pepper plant until late May, when the cages are removed. As a result, his pepper plants grew 7 feet tall and were still producing in mid-December. "By my count," wrote Watson in *National Gardening*, "we harvested up to sixty peppers per plant!"

It is ironic that some gardeners use reflective mulches to increase yield while others use shading. Experiments have been conducted to determine the effect of shading on fruit yield in peppers. In the early 1970s, Paul G. Schoch of the National Institute for Agronomic Research in Guadeloupe, French West Indies, grew two groups of Bell peppers in black plastic pots under identical conditions. One of the groups was shaded under black cloth between 10:00 A.M. and 4:00 P.M. each day. The black cloth permitted only 45 percent of the normal solar radiation to reach the leaves. After sixty days of this treatment, when the first flowers appeared, the plants were transplanted into open fields. The shaded plants had more fruits per plant, a greater mean weight per fruit, and a much greater total weight of fruits per plant. The results also suggest that pepper plants transplanted from greenhouses, where the light conditions are lower, will yield more than directly seeded plants will.

Some peppers grow well in shady conditions all year long. *Chiltepins* are usually found beneath "nurse" trees, especially mesquite, so these chile pepper plants are accustomed to low-light conditions. But

6.5   Simple Garden Shading

we have grown Arizona varieties of *chiltepins* in full sun in the Southwest with spectacular results. Potted *chiltepins* should not be grown in full sun or their leaves may yellow and drop.

Shading is also useful for some varieties, namely of the *chinense* and *pubescens* species, in the high, dry altitudes of the Southwest that have high levels of ultraviolet light. During the 1992 growing season, varieties of both of these species performed better and had higher yields under netting than they did in open, unshaded plots.

During the hottest days of July and August, many pepper plants lose more water by transpiration than can be taken up by the roots, no matter how wet the ground is. The results are wilting, flower drop, and sometimes even fruit drop. Antitranspirants, oil or wax emulsions sprayed on leaves to reduce water loss, are available. They do reduce water loss, but they do not increase yield or pod size. The simplest method of fighting water loss from transpiration is to increase the humidity around the plants by wetting thick layers of mulch such as grass clippings.

Peppers in Cool Climates

Pepper growers in colder climates in the United States and Canada and at high altitudes such as Colorado (which has a fifty-six-day growing season at 8,500 feet) face many challenges in producing a good crop: a short growing season, low night temperatures, unexpected frosts, and high sunlight intensity. Fortunately, there are solutions for these problems.

Handy Hints

In his garden in upstate New York (Zone 5), Ray Lagoe grows more than fifty varieties of chile peppers—everything from Habaneros to Tabascos to Serranos. Ray, who wrote about "Chilly Chiles" in *Chile Pepper* magazine, notes: "If you follow these guidelines and don't rush and plant too early, you should have the same excellent results I've had for years." His guidelines are:

- Select early maturing varieties.
- Start seed indoors eight to ten weeks before the last expected frost date.

- Plant seed in a sterile, soilless mix, and keep the seed at 75°F, under fluorescent light for between ten and twelve hours a day.

- Two weeks before transplanting seedlings into the garden, cover the rows with clear plastic mulch to warm the soil.

- Before planting, harden off the seedlings for two weeks or more by leaving them outside for increasingly longer periods of time each day.

- Transplant seedlings when daytime temperatures average 70°F and nighttime temperatures stay above 55°F.

- Soil pH should be 6.5; use a balanced fertilizer (5-10-5 or 10-10-10), but go easy on the nitrogen or you will have great-looking plants and no fruit.

- Cutworms can be a problem in northern gardens, so always protect seedlings with cardboard collars.

- Water during dry spells (at least two inches a week), especially after fruit-set.

Dick Worth, who grows eighteen varieties of peppers in Dauberville, Pennsylvania (Zone 6), says that a head start is the best strategy for gardening in cooler climates. "I planted Habanero seeds in flats under grow lights on February 15," he told us, "and transplanted the seedlings into four-inch peat pots on March 15. I kept the potted plants on a windowsill until the middle of April, when it was warm enough to transfer them into a cold frame. I put the potted plants into the garden on May 15."

The results? "I picked the first edible pods in the middle of August," Dick reported. "The mature plants were about 30 inches high and 30 inches wide, and each of them produced approximately fifty to sixty extremely hot fruits."

Site-Specific Planting

Cold weather gardeners need to pay particular attention to garden planning. Planting the peppers on the south side of ridges that run east and west in the garden will increase the growth rate because the soil facing the sun will be warmer than level soil is. Raised beds that slope toward the south can also be used. Sunken beds covered with polyethylene sheeting slit for ventilation will give plants a good start in cold weather.

Row Covers

In Connecticut, the problem is that the growing season for Bell peppers is too short to achieve good production of mature red and yellow pods. In 1987 and 1988, Martin Gent of the Connecticut Agricultural Experiment Station used floating row covers made from spun-bonded polypropylene. This light and porous material is draped directly over the plants and traps solar energy, warming the plants by 5°F during the day.

Gent transplanted seedlings of numerous Bell varieties on 20 April and covered them for eight weeks. He also transplanted seedlings on 23 May and covered them as well. The later transplants did not result in early production, but the results for the 20 April transplanting were good, with several varieties ('Golden Belle', 'Gypsy', 'Canape', and 'Park's Early Thickset') producing early yellow or red pods. Growth under the row covers increased the number of peppers by between 12 and 19 percent; however, the average weight of each pod decreased by between 5 and 15 percent. Gent concluded that row covers work well for gardeners in short growing seasons who need earlier maturing pods.

Polyethylene bed covers worked well at Uvalde, Texas. Researchers from Texas A&M University found that row covers tripled the early yield of New Mexican varieties. The use of row covers can bring in a crop between two and three weeks earlier than normal. Home gardeners can fashion row covers from clear polyethylene stretched over wire or wooden frames, or they can use clear, corrugated fiberglass.

Row covers are also available from mail-order companies and garden shops. The manufacturers of the Reemay row cover say that their product insulates plants against light frost and enables the grower to plant ten to fourteen days earlier. They also claim that their spun-polyester row cover extends the harvest by two to three weeks and keeps insects out—which would be a perfect way to avoid cross-pollination. Plastic row covers, which are really small row greenhouses called "tunnels," protect delicate plants from wind, cold, and snow—but not against insects.

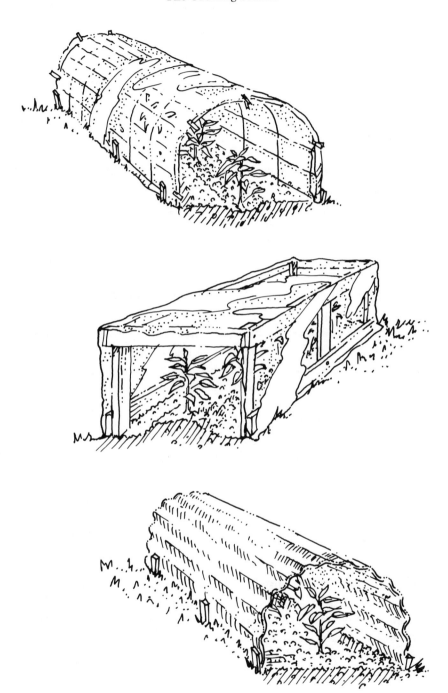

6.6   Row Covers

Warming the Ground and Extending the Season

In addition to mulches and row covers, there are other methods to warm the soil so that peppers can get a head start during a short growing season. Some gardeners grow their peppers inside automobile tires (or inner tubes) that are filled with water. The tire protects small plants from the wind and absorbs heat from the sun. The water warms both the soil and the air around the peppers and releases heat during cold nights. The open water in the tire may offer breeding sites for mosquitoes, so place a few drops of motor oil on the water. Many nurseries and garden supply shops sell flexible plastic rings that may be filled with water, serve the same purpose as the tires, and are more attractive.

Another soil-warming technique is to fill one-gallon plastic milk jugs with water and bury them halfway in the ground next to the plants. Solar radiation will heat the water, which will keep the ground warmer near the plants.

Reflector panels, made of wood and painted black or the color of aluminum, can be mounted on the north side of ridges that run east and west to reflect sunlight onto the plants and the ground. Such reflectors should be removed later in the summer when the weather heats up.

Microclimates in some regions seriously affect the length of the growing season. For example, in Albuquerque, certain parts of the valley are hit by early frosts but the higher elevations are not (cold air sinks). What often happens is that after an early frost, the weather will warm up sufficiently for another three weeks of growing. The problem is to keep the early frost from killing the plants. Short of using heaters, as citrus growers do, the best and easiest solution is to cover the plants. Many materials, such as cotton bed sheets, clear or black plastic sheeting, nylon netting, plastic row covers, and even large cardboard boxes, can be used, depending on the arrangement of the plants—and their size. Ideally, the thickest and most dense material will retain ground heat the most efficiently. Sometimes thick material is, however, heavy enough (especially if there is rain or snow) to break off branches. The choice of material depends on what is available, the amount of work involved in covering the plants, and the projected low temperature. If the temperature is expected to hover somewhere between 28°F and 32°F, the effort is probably worth it. If the temperature is expected to drop below 28°F, the effort will probably be wasted.

The commercial copy for a product called Wall O'Water claims that this product adds up to eight weeks to the growing season. Teepees of clear plastic eighteen inches high and filled with three gallons of water surround young plants and protect them from the wind and cold. The water in the teepees absorbs heat and releases it during the night. When the plants are mature and frost threatens, the water retains heat and releases it at night. When temperatures go below freezing, the water actually releases heat as it freezes, further protecting the plants.

Recommended Varieties

We have searched the information sent by various state cooperative extension services in the colder states to find the recommended varieties for their areas. Pepper growers in colder regions should contact their extension services for suggestions, then order as many seed catalogs as possible. High Altitude Gardens in Ketchum, Idaho, specializes in seeds and resources for cool weather gardening. The following suggestions are compiled from extension services in Alaska, Colorado, Idaho, Minnesota, and Vermont. The addresses of the seed sources are given in Resources. These varieties are probably the best for cooler climates, but are certainly not the only varieties that might be grown.

BELLS

'California Wonder': Field's, Gurney, Harris, Liberty, Nichols, Pinetree, Porter, Territorial Seed, Twilley

'Gypsy': Burpee, Field's, Gurney, Harris, High Altitude, Liberty, Nichols, Rocky Mountain Seed, Twilley

'Karlo': Seeds of Change

'Mexi-Bell': Burpee, Enchanted Seeds, Liberty, Park, Plants/Southwest, Porter, Rocky Mountain Seed, Tomato Grower's, Twilley

'Hungarian Yellow Wax Hot': Burpee, Gurney, Harris, High Altitude, Johnny's, Liberty, Park, Porter, Rocky Mountain Seed, Seeds of Change, Territorial Seed, Twilley

'Jalapa': Porter, Rocky Mountain Seed, Twilley

'Long Slim' Cayenne: Burpee, Enchanted Seeds, Field's, Liberty, Park, Porter, Redwood City Seed, Rocky Mountain Seed, Territorial Seed, Tomato Grower's

'Super Chili' Ornamental: Burpee, Enchanted Seeds, Field's, Gurney, Liberty, Nichols, Park, Porter, Shepherd's, Tomato Grower's, Twilley

CHAPTER 7

Pests and Problems

In 1987, Fish and Game Department authorities in New Mexico gave farmers permission to shoot deer out of season. The reason? The deer were raiding chile pepper fields—a heinous crime in our state. They ate two acres of pods and severely damaged three more acres (at a loss to growers of $4,000 an acre). Although such deer depredations are unusual, they show that peppers are susceptible to more than insects and disease. Reports of damage by mammals and birds are common. Cats often graze on pepper seedlings, chewing them down to the soil. Parakeets and other pet birds have been known to do this too. Dogs and pepper plants are not compatible. If allowed into the garden, dogs will dig up the plants or trample them. In one extreme case, a young Doberman ate the pods off a Cayenne plant! They have also been known to damage pepper plants by urinating on them. The urine turns the leaves yellow, causes them to curl into weird shapes, and stunts the plants. On lawns the problem is called "canine spotting syndrome."

David Plotnikoff, a food writer in San Jose, California, had lots of trouble with squirrels, which kept digging up his transplants. He finally built a frame over his peppers and stretched deer netting over it to keep out the squirrels. In south Texas, jackrabbits are a problem and must be fenced out of pepper fields. Roy Nakayama, the late chile pepper breeder, once reported that skunks were eating the pods in some of his fields.

Commercial growers occasionally report that birds, especially some varieties of blackbirds, damage the pods on their plants by pecking through them to eat the seeds. Even a small hole in a pod can lead to a bacterial infection. Birds are particularly attracted to the small, red pods of Piquins, Ornamentals, and Exotics, and eat them whole.

Most laws prohibit killing the animals and birds that raid peppers, so there are two general solutions to the problem: isolate the plants with fences or netting, or scare the pests away.

Diagnosing the Damage

Even under the best growing conditions, pepper plants may become diseased or infested. The correct diagnosis of a disorder is important in order to choose the proper treatment; the wrong treatment is expensive and senseless. Diagnosis by reading a description of the problem is difficult, especially for diseases. With practice and the information in this chapter, the gardener can, however, make an educated guess.

Diagnosing health problems in plants is a three-step process. Frequent examination of the pepper plants leads to the first step in the diagnosis: perceiving the problem. The next step is to determine the cause, and the final step is to choose an appropriate solution according to information gathered in the first two steps.

A thorough examination of the plants is necessary, so use a hand lens to look closely at unhealthy tissue. Are fungal spores, such as those of powdery mildew or anthracnose, present? Are leaf spots oozing a slimy material, possibly an indication of a bacterial infection? Are any insects present?

Root problems usually have nonspecific symptoms, such as wilting, yellowing, or dieback. The gardener will not always be able to determine the cause of the problem while investigating, and samples may need to be sent to a university or diagnostic laboratory for further testing. Laboratories are most useful for soil testing, microscopic tissue examinations, and culturing plant-disease organisms. The more information the gardener provides, the easier it is for a laboratory to find a solution. Follow the lab's instructions on how to prepare and ship the sample, and provide a copy of all the information collected.

Each state provides assistance for home gardeners. The cooperative extension service can help with a disorder because it has access to research information and resources of universities, the U.S. Department of Agriculture, and other federal agencies. Some county agent offices have a series of telephone tape recordings on various gardening topics.

Information gathered in the first two steps above is vital in deciding what control or management procedures are necessary. Remember the principles of integrated pest and disease management when making a plan. The final plan may be similar whether the problem is infectious or not. Integrated pest or infectious disease management is accomplished by cultural as often as by pesticidal methods.

Be diligent and keep detailed records of observations. Do not depend on your memory for important details such as when a symptom first appeared, when a problem was treated, weather conditions when the problem was observed, and which cultivars appeared more resistant or susceptible. A symptom may result from multiple causes, rather than from one isolated pathogen or environmental factor. Therefore, apply integrated diagnostics to diagnose and control the problem.

Nonliving (abiotic) and living (biotic) agents can disease and injure peppers. Nonliving factors that cause disease include extreme levels of temperature, moisture, light, nutrients, pH, air pollutants, and pesticides. Living pathogens that cause disease include fungi, bacteria, viruses, mycoplasmas, insects, and nematodes.

Two basic approaches to the control of pepper disease and pests are organic gardening techniques and synthetic (artificially produced) chemicals. Both methods have merits and can be used independently. A combination often provides the most effective method to prevent disease and pests. Organic insecticides include rotenone, pyrethrum, and microbial preparations such as *Bacillus thuringiensis* (BT). All the treatments listed in this chapter are not needed in all locations every year.

Disease can cause extensive losses in the yield and quality of peppers. Disease and insect control in the home garden must start before plants and seeds are planted. Plan a long-range program and record, from one year to the next, the location of plant types. This method will help in effective crop rotation, which is one way of minimizing root-rot disease caused by soil-borne pathogens.

Another important way to control disease is by using good cultural and sanitation practices. This includes proper soil preparation, fertilizing, watering, and the early detection and removal of infected plants. The latter is especially helpful if you wish to avoid using fungicides.

An equally important, but often overlooked, method of controlling disease is simply to plant disease-resistant varieties of peppers. Many are resistant to at least one virus, but some pathogens cause several viruses. Thus, multiple resistance must be incorporated for total protection. Two common pepper diseases, bacterial leaf spot and tobacco mosaic virus, are best controlled through resistant varieties.

Foliar disease is usually spread by splashing water. Therefore, foliage should be watered early in the day to allow it to dry before the evening hours. Proper plant spacing to provide adequate air movement around plants helps reduce the severity of disease. When it rains a lot, foliar diseases become difficult to control, even with fungicides, which should usually be applied at the first sign of disease.

The general principles of disease control can be summarized:

- Provide adequate space between plants. This allows good air movement and will help control diseases.

- Plant healthy seeds and transplants. Disease can be introduced by infested seed or plants. Careful inspection is recommended. Purchase transplants from a local, reputable, reliable source, such as a trusted garden center.

- Plant disease-resistant and -tolerant varieties when available.

- Use crop rotation: avoid planting the same or related crops in the same plot in successive years. Do not rotate tomatoes, eggplants, or potatoes to the sites where peppers were planted the year before. Most pathogens die when suitable hosts are absent.

- Water plants in the early morning so that the foliage will dry. Watering the plants in the evening will create ideal conditions for the development and spread of disease.

- Control insects early in the season because many of them transmit virus and bacterial disease to healthy plants. Aphids and leafhoppers transmit viruses and mycoplasmas from infected plants to healthy plants. Aphids feed on infected weeds, then move to the peppers, thereby introducing viruses that are spread in secondary cycles within the planting. In some instances, it only takes five to ten seconds of feeding by an aphid to infect a pepper plant.

• Use sanitation techniques. Dispose of diseased plants and frequently clean and disinfect equipment and benches. Control weeds around the garden area because many disease organisms survive on weeds and can be transferred to peppers by insects and wind. Be aware that perennial weeds can harbor reservoirs of destructive viruses over the winter.

For soilborne pathogens (*Verticillium*, *Fusarium*, *Pythium*, *Rhizoctonia*, and others), a chemical, such as metham sodium (Vapam), may be added to the soil. Where temperature and moisture favor disease, you may have to spray fungicides every five to seven days. Fungicides should not be the only control method. Some or all of the above-mentioned measures must be used.

The licensing, registration, and use of all pesticides are stringently restricted at both federal and state levels in the United States. Before a pesticide is applied to peppers, its package label should be reviewed to determine if it is allowed. Do not use *any* chemical that is not specifically labelled for peppers. If you have any doubts, consult the county agent or a responsible nursery person first.

Bacterial Diseases

Bacterial Soft Rot

Bacterial soft rot of pepper is caused by *Erwinia carotovora* pv. *carotovora*.

SYMPTOMS: It begins in the stem end of the fruit, but can occur through wounds on the pod. The internal tissue softens, and the pod turns into a watery mass. The pod also has a foul smell.

CONTROL: It is worst in wet weather because the bacteria are splashed from the ground onto the fruit. It can also be started by insect injury. Therefore, controlling insects helps prevent this disorder.

Bacterial Spot

Bacterial spot of pepper is caused by a bacterium, *Xanthomonas campestris* pv. *vesicatoria*, which also causes bacterial spot of tomatoes.

SYMPTOMS: Bacterial spot affects the above-ground parts of the plant. On young leaves, the spots are small, yellowish green, and slightly raised on the underside of the leaf. On older leaves, the spots are first dark, water soaked, and not noticeably raised. When spots are few, they may enlarge to one-eighth or one-fourth inch in diameter. These spots have dead, straw-colored centers with a dark margin. Severely spotted leaves turn yellow and drop. Infected seedlings often lose all but the top leaves of the plant.

The first signs of bacterial spot on fruits are small, raised, dark spots that are often surrounded by a water-soaked margin. The spots appear angular, for the bacteria spread along the veins. As the disease progresses, the spots may enlarge, turn black, and become rough, giving the fruit a scabby appearance.

CONTROL: The best control is crop rotation and the use of disease-free seed. The organism is seed-borne and, in some areas, can overwinter on diseased plant refuse in the soil. The main source of infection is infected seed. From infected seedlings the disease can spread rapidly during warm, rainy weather, especially when driving rain and wind have injured the plants. Marginal success in controlling the disease has come from using copper-based bactericides. Excessive use of copper may, however, retard growth.

Bacterial Wilt

Bacterial wilt is caused by *Pseudomonas solanacearum*.

SYMPTOMS: The disease begins with a wilting of leaves. After a few days, a permanent wilt results, with no leaf yellowing. A test for this bacteria is to cut the roots and lower stems, suspend them in water, and look for an exudate of milky streams of bacteria.

CONTROL: Plant clean seed and transplants and reduce the problem in the garden by discarding diseased plants.

Fungal Diseases

Anthracnose

Several species of the fungus *Colletotrichum* cause this disorder.

SYMPTOMS: Small, water-soaked, shrunken lesions are usually found on ripe pods. The lesions have dark fungal spores in them and a characteristic concentric-ring appearance.

CONTROL: Clean seed and crop rotation are important. If the disorder is severe, a fungicide may be needed.

Cercospora Leaf Spot (Frogeye)

Cercospora capsici causes this disorder.

SYMPTOMS: The brown, circular leaf lesions with small, light gray centers and a dark brown margin (the frogeye) are distinctive. Infected leaves commonly drop.

CONTROL: Clean seed and crop rotation are important. The disease is worst under humid conditions. Fungicides can help to manage it.

Damping-Off

Several fungi, among them *Pythium*, *Rhizoctonia*, and *Fusarium*, are associated with damping-off.

SYMPTOMS: Seedlings fail to emerge (preemergence damping-off), small seedlings collapse (postemergence damping-off), or seedlings are stunted (root rot and collar rot).

CONTROL: Treating the seed or the soil with a fungicide are the most common methods of control. Most commercially prepared soil mixes are free of these fungi. Good air circulation is important, so fans are helpful in greenhouses.

Fusarium Wilt

Fusarium oxysporum f.sp. *capsici* is the fungus that causes this disease.

SYMPTOMS: An initial slight yellowing of the foliage and wilting of the upper leaves progresses in a few days to a permanent wilt with the leaves still attached. Cut stem shows a browning, similar to verticillium wilt.

CONTROL: High temperatures and wet soil conditions favor the disease and it is most likely to occur in poorly drained areas. Good drainage is essential.

Gray Mold

Botrytis cinerea is the fungus that causes this disease.

SYMPTOMS: A sudden collapse of succulent tissues, such as young leaves, stems, and flowers. Gray powdery spore masses of the fungus occur on the surface of dead plant tissues.

CONTROL: High humidity favors the disease so plants should be widely spaced. If they can dry quickly the disease will be reduced. A fungicide may be used if the mold is severe.

Phytophthora Blight

This water mold, *Phytophthora capsici*, can invade all plant parts. The fungus may cause three separate disorders: foliar blight, fruit rot, or root rot. It spreads rapidly when humidity and temperatures are high and the soil is wet.

SYMPTOMS: Often called chile wilt, it differs from vascular wilts (the plugging-up of vascular tissues) caused by *Verticillium dahliae* and *Fusarium oxysporum*. Large plants wilt and die, leaving brown stalks and leaves and small, poor-quality fruits. If the fungus enters the roots, the plants cannot obtain enough water, may suddenly wilt, and eventually die. When the disease is severe, the fungus may attack main

7.1   Phytophthora Damage in a Chile Pepper Field

stems and branches, causing brown or black spots that kill that portion of the plant. The disease is most common in overwatered areas, such as low spots, and in heavy soils.

CONTROL: Chile wilt can be prevented by avoiding excess water. Do not allow water to stand in the garden, and when cultivating, build up the soil so that the plants are growing on a high ridge. Fungicides work against foliar blight and fruit rot, but not against root rot.

Powdery Mildew

The fungus that causes powdery mildew is *Leveillula taurica*.

SYMPTOMS: Chlorotic (yellowing) blotches or spots that may become necrotic (dead) with time. On the lower leaf surface, a white to gray powdery growth may exist. Leaf drop is common.

CONTROL: Fungicides may be needed. Other plants in the garden with powdery mildew should be removed.

Southern Blight

Sclerotium rolfsii is the fungus that causes southern blight.

SYMPTOMS: The leaves wilt suddenly but do not discolor at first. They may turn yellow later. The base of the stem is brown and decayed above and below the soil line. White fungus is visible at the base of the stem and on the soil around the base. Sclerotia, small brown spheres about the size of mustard seeds, can be found in the fungus.

CONTROL: Till deeply to bury the sclerotia, remove infected plants, and allow a plot to lie fallow for a couple of years. Soil fungicides may provide some control.

Verticillium Wilt

Two different species of fungi can cause this disease, *Verticillium dahliae* and *V. albo-atrum*.

SYMPTOMS: Plants first wilt, then usually shed many leaves, and finally die. If the stem is cut, a vascular discoloration is seen.

CONTROL: No resistant cultivars nor chemical controls are known. Solarization of garden soil has worked under certain conditions. Rotate crops, but not with eggplant, okra, or tomatoes.

White Mold

White mold, or sclerotinia disease, is caused by the fungus *Sclerotinia sclerotiorum*. It causes a wilt, rot, and blight.

SYMPTOMS: Any above-ground or below-ground plant part may blight or rot. At first, the affected area of the plant has a dark green, greasy, or water-soaked appearance. On stems, the lesion may be brown to gray. If the humidity is high, a white, fluffy mycelial (mold) growth appears. Lumpy areas appear in this white growth, which become hard and black as they mature. The hard, black bodies (sclerotia) form inside the stem or on the outside surfaces of the stem and other plant parts.

CONTROL: Control includes well-drained soil, proper plant spacing, crop rotation, and careful removal of all infected plants as soon as possible. Do not compost the plants or use them for mulch.

Viral Diseases

Viruses are extremely small and can only be seen with an electron microscope. Viruses alter the metabolism of plant cells, causing the plants to grow abnormally. This condition causes decreased yields and visible symptoms, such as distorted leaves, abnormally colored leaves, dead tissue, mottled or mosaic leaves or fruit, stunted plants, or curled leaves. One plant can be attacked by many viruses and may express many different symptoms. Viruses are transmitted from plant to plant by insects, aphids being the worst culprits, or by the grower in handling infected plants.

To help protect plants against tobacco mosaic virus, avoid using tobacco in any form. Gardeners who use tobacco should wash their hands with soap and water, rubbing alcohol, or milk before handling healthy plants. Early detection and removal of infected plants helps, but complete control is often difficult.

Mosaic viruses show up as an intermixture of light and dark green patches. The mottled areas have irregular outlines and may follow the main veins. Infected leaves are generally smaller than healthy leaves are, and are often slightly puckered and have curled edges. In severe cases, the leaves may become long, narrow, and twisted. Infected plants are usually more dwarfed and bushy than healthy plants are and have reduced yields. Distinguishing symptoms caused by mosaic diseases from those caused by abnormal pH, herbicide injury, nutritional deficiencies, damage caused by feeding mites or insects, and so forth may be difficult. No viricides exist that control plant viruses. To help reduce mosaic virus, plant virus-free seed, remove weeds, control insects, remove plants showing symptoms of the virus, and plant resistant varieties.

Alfalfa Mosaic Virus (AMV)

Aphids carry AMV, and peppers planted near alfalfa have a higher incidence of the disease.

7.2   Alfalfa Mosaic Virus Damage

SYMPTOMS: Plants are mildly stunted and have whitish blotches on the leaves. The infected area is bleached white and mottled. The fruit may be distorted.

CONTROL: Control aphids and avoid planting near alfalfa. Use resistant varieties if they are available.

Beet Curly Top Virus (BCTV)

Curly top is carried by leafhoppers.

SYMPTOMS: The most striking symptom is that the plants are stunted and yellow. They are also quite stiff and erect, and the leaves feel leathery.

CONTROL: The leafhoppers that carry the virus do not feed in shady locations, so plants may be partially shaded with muslin tents or by other means early in the season. Spraying or dusting with insecticide is justified only when control is needed for other insects.

Cucumber Mosaic Virus (CMV)

Aphids carry CMV.

SYMPTOMS: The plants become stunted and the foliage dull green, with a leathery appearance.

CONTROL: Control aphids and avoid planting peppers near cucurbits.

Pepper Mottle Virus (PeMV)

Aphids carry PeMV.

SYMPTOMS: Stunted plants, distorted fruit, and a diminished yield are symptoms.

CONTROL: Control aphids, practice good sanitation, and plant resistant varieties if they are available.

Potato Virus Y (PVY)

PVY is carried by aphids and has been called the most common pepper virus.

SYMPTOMS: Symptoms include mosaic and dark green vein-banding, crinkled, distorted leaves, and stunted plants.

CONTROL: Plant resistant varieties and control aphids.

Tobacco Etch Virus (TEV)

Aphids carry TEV.

SYMPTOMS: Mosaic and dark green vein-banding, distorted leaves, and stunted plants are the symptoms. Tabasco plants wilt and die.

CONTROL: Plant resistant varieties and control aphids.

Samsun Latent Tobacco Mosaic Virus (SLTMV)

SLTMV is spread mechanically, by hands touching an infected plant and then touching an uninfected plant.

SYMPTOMS: Typical symptoms include mild mosaic and leaf distortion. Pods develop rings, line patterns, and necrotic spots, and become distorted. Plants may be stunted.

CONTROL: Disinfecting hands with alcohol helps. Clean seed and crop rotation also help control the virus.

Tobacco Mosaic Virus (TMV)

TMV is spread mechanically, by hands touching an infected plant and then an uninfected plant.

SYMPTOMS: Mosaic and systemic chlorosis and leaf drop occur.

CONTROL: Disinfecting the hands with alcohol helps. Clean seed and crop rotation are the best prevention.

Tomato Spotted Wilt Virus (TSWV)

TSWV is carried by thrips that feed on various virus-infected perennial flowering plants commonly grown in gardens.

SYMPTOMS: Necrotic ringspots and leaf drop are symptoms.

CONTROL: Use clean seed and control thrips.

Insects and Other Pests

Insects are not usually a severe problem for peppers, but they do cause some damage. The most common are cutworms, aphids, pepper weevils, maggots, flea beetles, hornworms, and leafminers. Early in the season, cutworms cause the most damage to both seeded and transplanted peppers. Seedling peppers are subject to attack by flea beetles when the cotyledons emerge.

Green peach aphids can become numerous at any time, but are probably more prevalent during the summer.

Besides carrying disease, aphids cause stress by feeding on plant sap. Their honeydew gets on the fruit and leaves, and, if heavy enough, the resulting sooty mold growth can decrease photosynthesis.

Occasionally, loopers will feed on the foliage, exposing the pods to sunscald. Fall and beet armyworms, yellow-striped armyworms, and variegated cutworms may feed on pods. The beet armyworm will also feed on the foliage. The corn earworm feeds on pods, causing them to drop or become unmarketable.

Some insects in the garden will eat peppers but only if they have no alternative. The Colorado potato beetle, for example, generally prefers the other Solanaceous vegetables, particularly potatoes and eggplants.

Problem insects differ in each region. To control the insect population, and keep seedlings insect-free, inspect the plants daily, weed well around the peppers, dispose of diseased plants immediately, and use insecticides if necessary.

Common Cutworms

Many species of cutworms exist; they are the larvae of a large family of moths. They are dull gray, brown, or black, and may be striped or spotted. They are stout, soft-bodied, smooth, and up to one and one-fourth inches long. When disturbed, they curl up tightly.

DAMAGE: Cutworms attack only seedlings. They cut off the stems above, at, or just below the soil surface.

CONTROL: Tilling disturbs the overwintering places of the cutworm. When setting out plants in spring, place cardboard, roofing paper, plastic, or metal collars around the young stems, and push the collar one inch into the ground to stop the cutworms. Treating the soil with carbaryl (Sevin) before planting will also control cutworms.

7.3   Tomato Fruitworm (Corn Earworm)

European Corn Borers

Corn borer moths are active at night and hide during the day.

DAMAGE: The borer is hatched from eggs deposited on peppers by the corn borer moth. The larvae tunnel under the pepper pod calyx and feed inside the cavity.

CONTROL: Remove plant debris, especially cornstalks. The borer overwinters in corn stubble and emerges in the spring. *Bacillus thuringiensis* (BT), rotenone, and carbaryl (Sevin) are effective against the caterpillars.

Flea Beetles

Flea beetles are black and about one-sixteenth inch long.

DAMAGE: Young plants are severely damaged and full of holes.

CONTROL: Rotenone or carbaryl (Sevin) dust is effective. The flea beetle is repelled by shade.

Fruitworms

Fruitworms include the fall armyworm, beet armyworm, and tomato fruitworm (also called the corn earworm). At the larval stage, the worm is green, brown, or pink, with light stripes along the sides and on the back. It grows to one and three-fourths inches long.

DAMAGE: The fruitworm eats holes in fruits.

CONTROL: Fruitworms can be removed by hand. Rotenone, *Bacillus thuringiensis* (BT), or carbaryl (Sevin) dust are also effective.

Capsicum frutescens, a wild relative of the Tabasco from Costa Rica. (Photo by Dave DeWitt.)

A Cayenne plant. The mature red fruits are either ground into powder or used as a base for cayenne pepper sauces. (Photo by Paul W. Bosland.)

A Tabasco plant. The fruits mature from yellow to red: in the yellow stage, they are often pickled and canned; the red fruits are used extensively in hot sauces.
(Photo by Paul W. Bosland.)

Chile pepper *ristras* drying in the sun so they can be kept for winter, in the method used before commercial processing. A *ristra* hanging outside a home is a traditional sign of welcome: when travelers saw one, they knew they could stop in for a meal. No *ristra* meant that the household was low on staples and had no food to offer.
(Photo by Paul W. Bosland.)

Grasshoppers

Adults have front wings that are larger than the body and are held rooflike over the insect. The hind legs are long and adapted to jumping.

DAMAGE: Grasshoppers eat pepper foliage. They may destroy entire plantings.

CONTROL: Soil cultivation is useful because grasshoppers lay their eggs in the top three inches of soil. Birds often eat grasshoppers. Carbaryl (Sevin) dust is also effective.

Green Peach Aphids (Plant Lice)

These aphids are usually light green and soft-bodied. They cluster on the undersides of leaves or on stems.

DAMAGE: Aphids excrete a sticky liquid called honeydew, which creates spots on the foliage. A black fungus, sooty mold, may then grow on the honeydew. Severe infestations can cause wilting, stunting, curling, and leaf distortion.

CONTROL: Usually, aphid predators and parasites keep aphids down, but they can multiply quickly. Spray with insecticidal soap.

Grubs

Grubs are white to light yellow with dark brown heads. They are curved and one-half to one and one-half inches long. White grubs are the larvae of May beetles, live in the soil, and may take three years to mature.

DAMAGE: The larvae feed on roots and underground parts.

CONTROL: Till the soil repeatedly to uproot the grubs so the birds can eat them.

7.4   A Tomato Hornworm

Hornworms

The larval stage of the sphinx moth, tomato hornworms are large caterpillars. Their green bodies have diagonal lines on the sides and a prominent horn on the rear end. They can be up to four inches long.

DAMAGE: They eat foliage ravenously and can strip a pepper plant, killing it.

CONTROL: Hornworms are large enough to be removed by hand. Rotenone, *Bacillus thuringiensis* (BT), or carbaryl (Sevin) dust are effective.

Leafhoppers

Usually green, wedge-shaped, and up to one-eighth inch long, leafhoppers fly quickly when disturbed. Nymphs resemble the adults, but are smaller.

DAMAGE: The leafhopper spreads curly top virus and can cause hopperburn. Pepper leaves that turn yellow to brown on the tips and sides and become brittle are showing symptoms of hopperburn, which is rare in peppers.

148

CONTROL: Remove infested plants or plant parts immediately. Pyrethrum or carbaryl (Sevin) dust is effective.

Leaf Miners

The larva, which causes the damage, is yellow, about one-eighth inch long, and lives inside the leaves. The adult is a tiny black and yellow fly.

DAMAGE: The larvae make long, slender, winding mines under the epidermis of the leaves, which also turn blotchy.

CONTROL: Remove infested leaves. Sabadilla dust will also control leaf miners.

Pepper Maggots

The maggot is the larva of a fly. It is white or yellowish white, and about one-fourth to one-half inch long. Adults are yellow-striped flies about one-fourth inch long with dark bars on the wings.

DAMAGE: Maggots eat the core of the pepper pod, causing it to decay or drop from the plant.

CONTROL: Rotenone or malathion is effective.

Pepper Weevils

Black weevils are sparsely covered with gray or tan hairs. Larvae are white with brown heads.

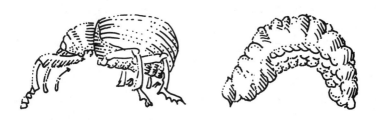

7.5   Pepper Weevil

DAMAGE: Both the grub and the adult weevil cause damage. The grub feeds on buds and the pods, feeding inside the fruit. Weevil larvae and excrement are left in the pepper fruit. The adult feeds on leaves, buds, and pods.

CONTROL: Destroy crop residue and weeds of the nightshade group to reduce the possibility of adult weevils overwintering. Plants should be dusted or sprayed weekly with carbaryl (Sevin) or diatomaceous earth.

Root-Knot Nematodes

Nematodes are microscopic worms that feed on the plant roots. Three species of root-knot nematodes cause serious damage to peppers: *Meloidogyne incognita*, *M. hapla*, and *M. arenaria*.

SYMPTOMS: Stunted plants and leaves wilting are evidence aboveground. Roots infected with root-knot nematodes have obvious swellings or galls. Injury is more severe in sandy soils.

CONTROL: Use resistant cultivars, crop rotation, and/or soil fumigants.

Slugs and Snails

Snails differ from slugs in that snails have shells.

DAMAGE: Plant parts are missing, and the pest leaves a shiny trail on the plant or the ground.

CONTROL: Slugs and snails can be trapped under boards. Pans of fresh beer can be placed in the garden to attract the pests. They fall in and drown. Chemical bait (metaldehyde) is also available.

Spider Mites

Spider mites are red arachnids almost too small to be seen with the naked eye. If the infestation is heavy, the underside of leaves will have webs on them.

DAMAGE: Spider mites cause leaves to curl downwards, like an inverted spoon, and leaves or fruits acquire a bronzed or russeted appearance. Mites can kill the plant if left uncontrolled.

CONTROL: In the early stages, these mites can be eliminated by washing the plant with a mild soap solution, then spraying the plant, including the undersides of leaves where the mites usually harbor, with water. Repeat this process weekly until the mites are gone. If the mite problem is very severe, a miticide can be sprayed on.

Stink Bugs

Stink bugs are green, blocky insects about half an inch long. Both the nymphs and adults damage plants.

DAMAGE: A cloudy spot, a whitish area with indistinct borders, appears on the fruits. Damage is similar to hail damage on fruit, but hail also tears leaves.

CONTROL: Sabadilla dust or carbaryl (Sevin).

Tarnished Plant Bugs

These insects have a greenish yellow to brown body, one-fourth inch long. There are yellow, brown, and black markings on the body and a yellow tinge at the end of each forewing.

DAMAGE: They inject a toxin when feeding on blossoms and buds, causing them to drop.

CONTROL: Sabadilla dust.

Thrips

Thrips are extremely small (between .04 and .06 inch long), winged insects that suck sap from plants. They can produce a new generation every two weeks.

DAMAGE: Leaves are distorted and curl upward (boat-shaped). The lower surface of the leaves develops a silvery sheen that later turns bronze.

CONTROL: Malathion, sulfur, and diatomaceous earth are effective.

Whiteflies

Whiteflies are harmful because they fly from one plant to another and quickly attack all peppers. They can also carry viruses to plants. These pests are white and about one-sixteenth inch long.

DAMAGE: Adult and young whiteflies feed on the undersides of leaves. They suck out the plant juices, causing the leaves to shrivel, turn yellow, and drop.

CONTROL: Get rid of infested plants that harbor the whiteflies. Soap solutions can be sprayed on the plant. Aerosol insecticides used for other flies will kill airborne whiteflies.

Other Problems

Blossom-End Rot

Blossom-end rot occurs when the plant is unable to take up adequate calcium, a condition caused by fluctuating soil moisture (drought or overwatering), excess nitrogen, or root pruning during cultivation. Wilting, overly dry soil, and lack of calcium exacerbate the problem.

SYMPTOMS: This disorder first appears as a water-soaked area. The tissue near the blossom end of pods has a brown discoloration. Spots elongate and become brown to black, dry and leathery. Discolored tissue shrinks until the affected area is flat or concave. Blemishes range from one-fourth-inch spots to three-inch-long elongated spots. Pods affected with blossom-end rot usually ripen prematurely. Frequently fungi will grow on and within the infected pods, but the fungi are not the cause of the initial problem.

CONTROL: Maintain a uniform supply of soil moisture through irrigation and avoid large quantities of nitrogen fertilizer. If manure is applied, turn it under in the fall (as early as possible) so it will be well rotted before planting time. Irrigate as necessary when the pods are developing rapidly. Some sources suggest adding calcium chloride to the soil to boost calcium, but we would discourage this practice in the Southwest, where the soils usually have too many salts.

Herbicide Injury

A hormone-type herbicide, such as 2,4-D (Weed-B-Gon), can cause distorted leaves. Other herbicides may cause chlorosis, necrosis, or lesions.

CONTROL: Control the spray drift of herbicides when applying them or simply avoid using herbicides near pepper gardens.

Mutations

Mutations can be mistaken for both herbicide damage and viral infection.

SYMPTOMS: Symptoms include leaf distortion, variegation in leaves, and fruit deformity.

CONTROL: No control is necessary. The pods of interesting mutants may be sent to the Capsicum Genetics Cooperative, Box 30003, Dept. 3Q, NMSU, Las Cruces, NM 88003.

Pod Drop

Excessive nitrogen, heat stress, or insufficient water will cause pods to drop.

SYMPTOMS: Immature pods drop off the plant.

CONTROL: Avoid overfertilizing and underwatering. When the condition is corrected, the plant will resume flowering and fruiting.

Salt Problems

Young seedlings may be "pinched off" at the soil line because of large quantities of salt in the soil. A young seedling can die when light rains move the salt to the tender roots.

CONTROL: Control salt problems by avoiding planting in saline soils. Irrigate heavily before planting so that the salt is washed down below the root area.

Sunscald

Sunlight causes the problem. Interestingly enough, the smaller-podded varieties with erect fruits are not as susceptible to sunscald as are the large-podded varieties, such as Bells and New Mexicans. Mature green fruits are the most sensitive.

SYMPTOMS: A necrotic or whitish area appears on the fruit, on the side exposed to afternoon sun. Often fungi, such as *Alternaria* spp., grow on the affected areas.

CONTROL: Keep pods shaded by the plant's leaves or by screening. Harvest the fruits carefully, and avoid stress to the plant from water, nitrogen, or nematodes.

7.6   Sunscald

Wind Injury

In most cases, pepper plants can withstand strong winds without significant injury.

SYMPTOMS: Some larger plants may snap off at the soil line, where callus tissue has formed, if the wind whips the plant back and forth in hard, crusty soil.

CONTROL: Control the problem by erecting wind screens.

CHAPTER 8

Potted Peppers
and Advanced Techniques

All varieties of peppers can be grown in containers, but usually they fruit faster and yield more when planted in the garden. Potted peppers dry out faster, drop blossoms, and have a tendency to lose their vigor after a season or two. Peppers grow better in the garden because the plants' roots are less restricted and there is a better microclimate—namely a cooler and moister environment.

There are, however, many advantages to growing peppers in containers. People who live in apartments and townhouses without gardens can grow peppers and other plants on their balconies, patios, or even in a closet under lights. Fresh pods from potted peppers are available all year long. Because the peppers can be moved around easily, they can be used as patio plants and ornamental houseplants. They can be rescued from heavy downpours or hail, or moved to areas of varying light levels. In pots, peppers are easier to isolate for breeding or for producing pure seed. Treasured varieties can be wintered over in a greenhouse or sunroom and returned to the garden the following year.

It seems to us that pepper gardening is becoming a popular hobby in the United States. Some enthusiasts become so fond of their potted peppers that they turn them into pets. They give them nicknames, take pictures of them to send to relatives and friends, and freely share their pods. This kind of behavior seems to be peculiar to pepper growers.

During our research for this book, we did not come across any studies done on potted peppers, so we've had to depend entirely on our own experiences and those of gardeners across the country. Fortunately, we've been in contact with a number of pepper hobbyists.

Choosing the Containers

Virtually anything that will hold soil can be used to grow peppers. If you are using containers to expand the size of your garden rather than to bring the plants indoors, then size and appearance are not a problem and you can use fairly large containers such as plastic trash cans, wooden boxes or barrels, styrofoam picnic coolers, or the large plastic, fiber, or metal pots used by greenhouses for shrubs and trees. For outdoor growing, the ideal size for containers is five gallons or larger.

If you are growing peppers in containers to winter them over, to turn them into perennials, or for breeding, smaller, more attractive containers should be used. We have had peppers in containers ranging in size from a plastic pot with a four-inch diameter to a barrel with a twenty-two-inch diameter. With a few exceptions, the larger the container, the larger the pepper plant will grow. Smaller containers restrict root growth, which limits foliage and flower production, but they are recommended for gardeners wishing to grow *bonsai* peppers. Remember that smaller containers will require more frequent watering, and that lighter-colored pots will reflect more solar energy and keep the roots of the plant cooler.

Gardeners can use their imaginations when selecting containers. For example, Diane Chamberlain reports good success in growing a

8.1   Potted Peppers

8.2   Various Containers for Growing Peppers

'Pepperoncini' in a hanging pot in her kitchen window when she lived in Japan. "It usually had peppers hanging on it," she said, "and I used them for cooking."

Varieties to Grow

At the risk of overgeneralizing, we believe that the smaller-podded varieties adapt best to container growing—especially to the smaller pots. During our experiments over six years, we had the best luck with *chiltepins*, Tabascos, and Ornamentals.

By far the best *annuums* we have grown in pots are *chiltepins*. From seeds collected by Jim Raney of Douglas, Arizona, in his back-yard, we raised a *chiltepin* that grew to an amazing 5½ feet tall in one season in a twelve-inch pot and produced a good yield of bright red, spherical pods. Our Mexican *chiltepins*, from seeds provided by Antonio Heras-Duran of Cumpas, Sonora, grew much more slowly, and the plants (in six- and eight-inch pots) barely topped a foot in one season. Three years later, the plants in the same pots were the same

8.3 Potted Peppers in a Greenhouse

size, but one that had been transplanted into an eleven-inch pot doubled in height. They respond well to pruning and can be fashioned into *bonsai* shapes. They still flowered and produced well after four years in pots.

At the end of the 1989 season, we dug a Tabasco plant out of the garden and put it in a twelve-inch pot. It spent the winter in the greenhouse and retained all its leaves, while other peppers in the greenhouse (including the *chiltepins*) dropped most of them and had to be pruned back. After the last frost the following spring, we placed it outside in full sun. It grew slowly and it yielded considerably fewer pods than it had when growing in the garden. It remained, however, an attractive, healthy plant, yielded well, and lived for three seasons in a pot before it lost vigor and died.

In 1989, we grew four different varieties of Habaneros in pots and they all did poorly. The same varieties, from Belize, Jamaica, Costa Rica, and Cuba grew slowly but yielded many more fruits in the garden. We repeated the experiment with two varieties of Habaneros in pots, and they performed much better, although the yield from the potted Habaneros was less than that of those planted in the garden.

All of the *ajís* did well in pots, even the ones that were wintered over in the greenhouse. The larger pods worked better for cooking as they were meatier and had a more distinct aroma.

Rocotos that were dug out of the garden and wintered over in the Albuquerque greenhouse had skimpy yields the following year, although a plant that had been grown from seed in the garden produced perhaps twenty pods. *Rocoto* leaves, which are quite pubescent, burn easily in the full New Mexico sun, so we had to shade them or grow them where they received only morning sun. In the Las Cruces greenhouse, they managed to survive in pots and produced well.

Most gardeners report that the New Mexican varieties do not respond well to containers unless they are grown in very large tubs or barrels. Consider, however, the adaptation of a New Mexican pepper at the offices of the *Chile Pepper* magazine. In the fall of 1991, Annette Hill discovered a volunteer growing beneath the *ristra* hanging outside the office door. She transplanted it to a six-inch pot and placed it in indirect light in the front office. Every day throughout the winter, after the air had warmed up, she placed it outside for a few hours of sun. The plant adopted a sprawling habit, seemed to thrive, and Annette babied it by washing off spider mites by hand. In the spring, the plant flowered and set fruit. Eventually the pods grew 2 inches long, but then started to dry out. In effect, Annette transformed the New Mexican pepper into an ornamental.

Techniques

One of the biggest problems with container gardening is the tendency for the plants to dry out and wilt between regular waterings. The major cause is transpiration, which is greater than one might expect even when the plant has a well-developed root system. Another cause of drying is evaporation from the top of the soil, which can be controlled with a mulch of grass clippings—but then it's hard to see how wet the soil is. The third cause is the type of soil chosen for the container.

Drainage and Soil

Good drainage is essential regardless of the type of container chosen for growing peppers. The containers should have large drain holes. To prevent soil from washing out of the holes, plug them with irregularly shaped stones. Some early sources suggest placing a three-inch layer of gravel to aid in drainage, but this practice is discredited today. Do not place the container in a jardiniere or in a saucer because of the risk of the roots sitting in water. Indoors, where saucers are a necessity, make sure the pot doesn't sit in water.

It is commonly believed that commercial potting soil is the best choice for containers because many garden soils contain too much clay for use in pots. Commercial potting soils often contain so much sand, perlite, and milled sphagnum moss that they drain too fast and dry out too quickly.

Some gardeners simply dig soil out of the garden and put it in a pot. Most pepper gardeners add some garden soil to a mix that includes commercial potting soil and other soil expanders. We have had good luck with the following formula: one part perlite, one part sand, one part vermiculite, three parts commercial potting soil, and three parts garden soil. Another good mixture is one part loamy soil, one part peat moss, and one part sand. Daphne Gould of Boston reports excellent results with a mixture of two parts compost, one part perlite, and one part garden soil, mulched with grass clippings. Gardeners will have to make some mixes with their own garden soil and judge for themselves which work best. Many sources suggest pasteurizing garden soil before using it in a pot, but that is a tedious process that tends to smell up the kitchen.

Location

Outdoors, peppers in containers seem to do best in partial shade or where they receive full sun only in the morning. There is a tendency for pots in full sun to absorb solar radiation and heat up the roots too much. If the pots are quite large, painted white or the color of aluminum to reflect solar energy, and are well mulched, many varieties will thrive in full sun. Indoors, the plants will be partially shaded by the movement of the sun, so place them in the sunniest window: usually an east or west window in the summer; a south window in the winter.

Fertilizing

Peppers in pots generally need a little more feeding than those growing outdoors in aged manure. About once a week early in the growing season use a balanced liquid fertilizer, such as 10-10-10, diluted even more than the instructions suggest. Fish emulsion seems to work for organic gardeners. Osmocote slow-release fertilizer is a good choice. It does not burn the plants and provides a steady supply of nutrients. If the growth of the potted pepper seems more vigorous than that of the same variety in the garden, or if blossoms are dropping, stop using the fertilizer. If blossom-drop continues, too much nitrogen has been applied, and the pot should be flushed by running a lot of water through it.

Problems

One of the biggest problems with growing peppers indoors is pets. The plants are chewed by cats, dogs, and birds. Some gardeners put netting over their peppers to keep the cats off, but then they can't see their favorite plants. Another problem with growing peppers indoors or in greenhouses is that they are more susceptible to the usual houseplant attackers: spider mites, whitefly, and aphids. See chapter 7 for methods of dealing with these pests.

Adequate light is needed in the winter, or the plants will cease flowering and begin to drop leaves. Jeff and Nancy Gerlach report that *rocotos* and other varieties grow well in the south-facing window of their office in Albuquerque. The light and heat were sufficient for the peppers to continue producing pods all winter long. In our north-facing greenhouse in Albuquerque, the peppers went into dormancy and lost many of their leaves.

Artificial Light for Peppers

In the March/April 1991 issue of *Chile Pepper* magazine, Cap Farmer, a pepper hobbyist in Richmond, Virginia, wrote: "I don't have to worry about winter freezes or heating a greenhouse because I grow all my chiles indoors, under lights!" Nancy and John Pierce of New Earth Indoor/Outdoor Garden Center in Shepherdsville, Kentucky, feel the same way. "Our indoor hydroponic chile peppers yield more and grow faster than soil-grown chiles," they told us. "Chiles are fairly easy to grow, tend to be high-yielding, and are always a lot of fun."

Types of Lights

The least expensive way to set up an indoor pepper garden is with fluorescent tubes. They are relatively efficient, cost little to set up, and a standard fixture accepts two forty-watt tubes. The number of fixtures depends on the size of the growing area, and they can also be placed vertically in corners for sidelighting. The major problem with fluorescents is that the intensity of light falls off very rapidly as a function of distance. The tops of the plants must remain between two and four inches below the tubes. Standard cool-white fluorescent tubes can be used, but many gardeners prefer the Sylvania Gro-Lux light, with its pink and purplish light, high-intensity output lights, or Vita-Lites, which provide almost 92 percent of the spectrum of natural sunlight.

The Pierces report: "Our research indicates that the color spectrum only minimally—if at all—affects plant growth. The biggest factor in plant performance is *enough* light, especially for plants setting flowers and fruit." To avoid the problem of low light levels on the lower foliage, serious pepper gardeners should use high-intensity discharge (HID) lamps. They are very similar to the mercury- or sodium-vapor lamps used to light city streets and come in two basic types, metal halide and high-pressure sodium. They use more electricity than fluorescent tubes do.

Metal halide lamps have a spectrum like that of the bright midday sun; high-pressure sodium lamps have the spectrum of the early morning or late afternoon sun, which, according to Cap Farmer, promotes flowering. The high-pressure sodium lamp emits more lumens of light than a metal halide lamp does. One word of warning: This equipment is identical to that used to grow marijuana indoors. The Drug Enforcement Administration has been known to subpoena the records of stores selling indoor growing equipment and to pay visits to their customers. There will be no problem as long as you are growing peppers—the legal high.

Reflectors

Either paint the plant growing room white or line it with white trashbags to reflect and diffuse light. Aluminum foil and mylar reflect light but do not diffuse it and, unless they are applied evenly, without wrinkling, cause numerous hot spots. Line the floors with white plastic to protect them from spills when watering.

Varieties

According to Cap Farmer, "the miniature varieties seem to do the best under lights, and I've had good success with 'Ethiopian' and 'Black Dallas'." Other peppers recommended for growing under lights are 'Thai Hot', 'Super Chili', and varieties of Piquin, such as *chiltepin*.

Growing Hints

The containers, soil mix, and fertilizing should be the same as those for other potted peppers. The Pierces told us that "indoor pepper gardeners will benefit from an eighteen-hour light cycle rather than a twelve-hour light cycle. Think of it this way: Chiles are long-day plants, yielding best during the long days of summer. They are not photo-period sensitive."

Peppers as Perennials

In 1753, the great Swedish botanist Linnaeus divided the *Capsicums* into two species: *frutescens* (perennial) and *annuum* (annual). It was commonly believed then that peppers that were not perennial belonged in a separate species, and it was not until 1923 that L. H. Bailey of Cornell University argued that *annuum* plants grown in a green-house did indeed become perennial and woody. We know today that all peppers are perennials—its just that some varieties like the idea better than others do.

Cal Dennler, a pepper aficionado in east Texas, has a six-year-old potted Serrano, so he knows how to grow perennial peppers. His technique is to dig the plants out of the garden and overwinter them in the greenhouse. "The strange thing is," he told us, "that they seem to do better if a frost nips them and I cut back the roots and above-ground growth. I plant them bare-root like a rose or a dormant tree."

But some peppers, especially the larger-podded varieties, resist becoming perennial. They tend to keep the annual cycle and stop flowering, drop leaves, and often die. This happens because some plants are determinate—they grow to a certain point and then stop. Other varieties grow well for a few years, then suffer a loss of vigor and produce fewer pods each year until they shut down and die. The decline would seem to be the result of old age, but could be related to environmental conditions such as root cramping. In some cases loss of vigor can be reversed by removing the pepper from the pot, trimming the roots, and replanting it in a larger container. In all cases, during the winter peppers respond best to as much light as they can get.

Perennial peppers respond well to pruning and *bonsai* peppers with special shapes, such as a single stalk and canopy, can be created. For bushier shapes, encourage multiple stems and prune back regular growth. Peppers do not respond well in traditional shallow *bonsai* pots.

Hydroponic Techniques

The term *hydroponics*, which means water culture, is generally used to describe any of several methods of growing plants without soil, and the concept is not new. In fact, researchers have been using this technique for more than a hundred years. But hydroponics is not a simple method for growing peppers, and is recommended only for dedicated gardeners. Commercial hydroponic systems are available, but all are expensive, complicated, and require considerable labor and maintenance.

Hydroponics is rarely superior to soil culture. To ensure satisfactory growth, plants require four components: sufficient light, proper temperature, adequate ventilation, and a balance of nutrients. The light, temperature, and ventilation are the same whether the pepper plants are grown in containers with soil or with liquid nutrients. But, because the water used in soilless culture is devoid of essential nutrients, they must be supplied. Commercially available fertilizer mixtures may be used, or nutrient solutions can be prepared from chemical salts.

Nutrient Solutions

The most widely used and generally successful nutrient solution is one developed by D. R. Hoagland and D. I. Arnon of the University of California, and many commercial mixtures are based upon their formula. A simple solution may be made from the following chemicals; each measurement is for level teaspoons of the chemical dissolved in five gallons of water:

Monopotassium phosphate	1
Sodium nitrate	1
Calcium chloride	1
Magnesium sulfate (Epsom salts)	2½

This nutrient solution provides only the major (macro) elements. In most cases, it is necessary to add microelements such as iron, manganese, boron, copper, zinc, and molybdenum to the solution. The formulae for the two essential microsolutions are given below.

SOLUTION NUMBER 1. In two quarts of distilled water, dissolve one teaspoon each of boric acid, zinc sulfate, and manganese sulfate and one-eighth teaspoon of copper sulfate. One or two teaspoons of this microsolution can be added to each five-gallon quantity of the macrosolution.

SOLUTION NUMBER 2. In two quarts of distilled water, dissolve one teaspoon of iron chloride. Add this mixture to the macrosolution at the rate of seven teaspoons to each five gallons of the macrosolution.

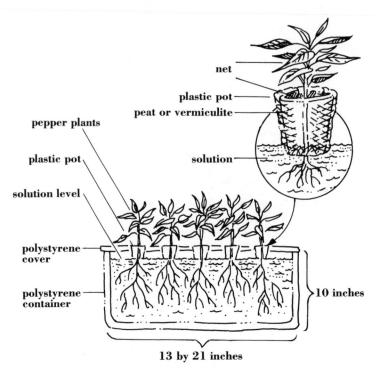

net

plastic pot

peat or vermiculite

pepper plants

plastic pot

solution

solution level

polystyrene cover

polystyrene container

10 inches

13 by 21 inches

8.4 A Simple Hydroponic System

The Growing System

An inexpensive, noncirculating hydroponic system designed by the Asian Vegetable Research and Development Center can be constructed from a polystyrene container (a soda or beer cooler). This container insulates the nutrient solution and maintains a relatively stable temperature. It holds a large volume of water, which helps maintain pH, nutrient levels, and electrical conductivity.

The combined macro- and micronutrient solution is added to a depth of four to eight inches below the top. A layer of nylon window screening is placed about one-half inch above the surface of the nutrient solution. This screen induces rapid lateral root growth and branching, promotes plant growth, and anchors the plant.

The polystyrene cover should be placed on the container to exclude light and prevent algae growth. Fifteen three-inch holes are made in the cover, and suitable plastic pots, with the bottoms removed and replaced with a circle of nylon screening to hold peat or vermiculite, are set in these holes and rest on the nylon screening in the large container. Pepper transplants that have been grown in peat or vermiculite are placed in these pots, and the pots are filled with additional peat or vermiculite. Immediately after transplanting, hand-water the pots with the nutrient solution to avoid transplant shock and wilting.

The nutrient level in the container will be reduced by evaporation, transpiration, and absorption by the root systems. Do not add large quantities of the nutrient solution at any one time—the level should be increased by no more than four inches. Pepper plants have grown well with a six-inch air space below the screen once the roots are established in the nutrient solution. The upper part of the root systems absorbs enough oxygen for aeration, while the lower part absorbs water and nutrients.

If the container is placed outside, a clear plastic cover should be set over it to protect the peppers and to prevent rainwater from entering the container. If the container is placed under artifical lights, the lights should be adjusted in the same way they are for peppers grown in containers with soil.

Pepper Breeding

Breeding peppers to create new varieties and improve old varieties is enjoyable and easy. The techniques of crossing varieties are easily learned and gardeners experiment with many different pepper types. Generally, amateur plant breeders work with traits that are fairly easy to change, such as fruit shape, fruit color, pungency, or plant size.

To breed peppers successfully, some knowledge of plant reproduction is important. A detailed discussion of this topic is beyond the scope of this chapter, but we will describe the basic techniques.

Plant Reproduction

Plants reproduce in two ways, asexually and sexually. Asexual, or vegetative, reproduction occurs without the fusion of reproductive cells. A strawberry that produces runners that take root and form new

8.5　Rooting Cuttings

plants is reproducing asexually. Plants originating from asexual reproduction are usually identical with the parent plant. Asexual reproduction can also be accomplished artificially by means of cuttings.

To reproduce pepper plants from cuttings, use a sterile knife and cut a non-woody branch section that has at least six leaves. Just above the end of the cutting, make a shallow incision in what is now the stem. Dip the end of the cutting in a rooting hormone powder such as Rootone to just above the incision and then place it in a rooting medium such as vermiculite in plastic cell packs. The best results occur when the cuttings are gently misted (see figure 8.5). Some cuttings will die, but some will take root. Check them periodically. When a cutting has formed a root ball it can be transplanted.

Sexual reproduction involves the union of male and female gametes. From this union, a seed is produced. Because of genetic recombination, plants originating from seed can be quite different from the parent and from each other. Plant breeders can therefore develop new varieties with sexual reproduction.

FLOWERS. Flowers of peppers are perfect (or complete) in the sense that each flower has both male and female organs. The sexual organs are easy to distinguish, so crossing peppers is relatively easy. Pollination is the transfer of pollen from an anther to a stigma. When the anther is mature, it opens and releases pollen. Pollen may be transferred in two ways: cross-pollination and self-pollination. In cross-pollination, the pollen is transferred from an anther of one plant to a stigma of another plant. In self-pollination, the pollen is transferred from an anther to the stigma of the same flower, or to the stigma of another flower on the same plant.

Early botanists grew peppers in greenhouses. Without insects, the peppers self-pollinated. Therefore, in earlier literature, peppers were considered to be self-pollinating. Cross-pollination is, however, quite common in peppers grown outdoors.

Other studies indicate that between 30 and 70 percent of pepper flowers can cross-pollinate, depending on location and season. Cross-pollination in peppers is enhanced by the structure of the pepper flower because the extended styles and the presence of nectar encourage insects.

Fertilization is the uniting of two gametes or reproductive cells. After resting on the stigma, the pollen develops a tube that grows downward through the style and into the ovule. Male and female gametes unite in the ovary. After fertilization, the ovule begins to develop and the result is a seed.

Plants, like animals, inherit traits from their parents. The reasons that different traits are inherited by the offspring of the same parents may be explained by the laws of heredity. These laws make it possible to predict the number of offspring that will inherit a certain trait. When the gametes unite in the ovule, each contributes one gene for each trait, so the new seed has two genes for each trait. Various combinations of the many genes inherited determine traits of the following generations.

We cannot always distinguish the genes a plant contains by just looking at it or tasting its pods. A pepper may contain genes for pungency and nonpungency, but only the pungency gene is manifest in the pods. Nevertheless, some of the plant's offspring will inherit the gene for nonpungency, and will pass it on to the following generations. This was the case with the cultivar 'NuMex Conquistador', a mild New Mexican variety that was an offspring of 'New Mexico

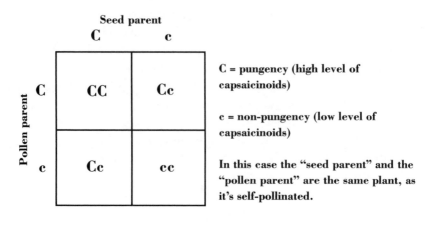

C = pungency (high level of capsaicinoids)

c = non-pungency (low level of capsaicinoids)

In this case the "seed parent" and the "pollen parent" are the same plant, as it's self-pollinated.

8.6   A Punnet Square

6-4', a pungent pepper. The plant breeder was not aware that the parent had any genes for nonpungency and produced the mild variety by accident.

By observing (and recording) the offspring's different traits, growers can discover the genes of the parent plants and how the genes interact. If a self-pollinated plant produces offspring that are identical to itself, it has bred true. The offspring of a cross are called the first filial (F_1) generation. If the first-generation offspring (F_1) are not all identical to the parent, the parent is segregating for the traits. If two true-breeding plants are crossed, one having two genes for pungency and the other having two genes for nonpungency, each F_1 plant inherits a gene for pungency and one for nonpungency.

When F_1 plants are self-pollinated, or selfed, their genes can combine in four different ways. The offspring resulting from the self-pollination of F_1 generation are called the second filial or F_2 generation. A chart to show this crossing is called a Punnet square. As figure 8.6 shows, one seed will have two genes for pungency, two seeds will have one gene for pungency and one gene for nonpungency, and one seed will have two genes for nonpungency. This ratio is based on large numbers and if only a few seeds are planted, the ratio may vary. If a seed contains two genes for the same trait, color for instance, it is pure for that trait.

Cross-pollination is usually necessary if we are to develop new varieties. Once a trait is fixed (once the plant breeds true for a specific trait), selfing the plant and its offspring will ensure that that trait continues to appear. Sometimes traits such as those for yield, earliness, or level of pungency cannot be fixed.

Growers may wish to breed for more than one trait. Some traits that are quite easy to change are those for plant size, fruit shape, fruit size, and the colors of immature and mature fruit. Some characteristics, such as yield and fruit size, are governed by many genes. Because there are two genes for each trait in each parent, many offspring will have to be grown before one will appear with all the desired traits. Even to replace only one trait with a more desirable one, the grower may have to raise many plants to avoid any changes in other traits.

HYBRIDS. F_1 hybrids are often mentioned in seed catalogs and breeding programs. These varieties are the result of crosses between two pure lines, with the purpose being to combine desirable traits of separate varieties. Some characteristics obtained in this way are increased vigor, increased yield, uniformity, and earliness. Seed taken from the mature hybrid pods will not produce peppers true to type, and numerous plants unlike the parent will result. Therefore, saving seed from hybrids is seldom worthwhile.

Tools

Equipment required for plant breeding is relatively inexpensive and easy to use. The basic items include rubbing alcohol, a pair of narrow-pointed forceps, a spear needle (a small scalpel), a hand lens, a pencil, string tags, and a notebook. The notebook will be used to record the parents' characteristics, as well as the performance of the resulting seedlings. Refer to figure 6.3 when pollinating pepper flowers.

SELF-POLLINATION. If you are going to self a pepper to produce pure seed, you must keep insects away from the flower. Growing the peppers in a greenhouse is the simplest way of doing that. Cages to isolate peppers being grown outdoors from insects can be made from any netting material, including drapery backing and nylon window screening. The entire plant can be caged, or just a branch. A simpler technique is to enclose a flowering branch in a small paper bag for a week. After the flowers have selfed, remove the bag and tag the pods

8.7　A Caged Pepper Plant

as selfed. Another technique is to place a gelatin capsule over the flower bud. This will keep the flower closed until it has selfed. As the fruit grows, it pushes the capsule off. Again, tag the selfed pods to distinguish them from others that might have been insect-pollinated.

CROSS-POLLINATION. Extremely high temperatures or moist conditions are harmful to pollen. For best results, pollinate plants on dry days during the cool morning hours. Crosses can be made at any time during daylight, but the best time is between one hour after sunup and approximately 11:00 A.M. The main objective in crossing is not to let the flower self-pollinate, which would make it useless for experimentation.

Prepollination is the technique used to avoid self-pollination, and it should begin before the flower opens. Peppers bloom over a period of time, and even if some of the flowers on a plant have bloomed before they are prepared for crossing, others will not have opened. Choose flower buds that are one to two days from opening. These buds are plump and white. Using forceps, remove the petals and sta-

8.8   A Crossing Tag

mens (this is called emasculation), leaving the calyx and pistil (the female organ). Use a magnifying glass for more accurate emasculation. From the male parent, either pull the anther from an opened flower and *gently* touch the anther to the stigma to transfer pollen, or take the spear needle, glean pollen from the anther, and place that on the stigma. Label the pollinated flowers with a string tag, and record on the tag the mother plant, the father plant, and the pollination date.

Because peppers are not wind pollinated, and insects will not visit the flower after the petals are removed, no other flower protection is necessary. After five to seven days, the flower will fall off if the cross did not take. Otherwise, the fruit will grow and mature and can be picked when it has reached the mature fruit color. Several flower buds should be pollinated at one time to increase the chance that the cross will take. To reduce cross-pollination, the tools must be disinfected with rubbing alcohol after each use. The alcohol must dry out on the tools before they are used again, or it will kill the pollen or ruin the stigma.

Most pepper types in this book belong to the species *C. annuum*. Any *C. annuum* pepper can be crossed with any other *C. annuum*. More exotic crosses, such as Habanero with Bell pepper or Tabasco with Jalapeño, are difficult because Habaneros and Tabascos belong to different species from Bells and Jalapeños. *C. annuum* and *C. frutescens* will cross reciprocally with *C. chinense*, producing partially fertile hybrids. The crossability of *Capsicum* species and the fertility of their offspring is discussed in chapter 6.

In Vitro Culture

The crossing barriers between species can be overcome by making numerous crosses or through the novel techniques of in vitro culture. In vitro culture is similar to asexual propagation, but the plant parts are grown on nutrient media under sterile conditions. The plant parts used are embryos, organs, tissues, cells, and protoplasts (cell protoplasm). At present, not all of those plant parts can be used to regenerate peppers. Embryo culture, meristem (growing point) culture, and anther culture have been successful; protoplast regeneration of peppers has not.

Disease

Most fungal, bacterial, and viral pathogens can be transferred from mother plant to seed. Careful inspection of the mother plants is essential for producing pathogen-free seed. Fortunately, seed crops are usually grown in arid areas where insects that carry pathogens are scarce and bacterial and fungal diseases minimal.

Saving Seed

Regardless of whether seeds are produced through self-pollination or cross-pollination, they must be preserved until the next growing season or even later. On the average, pepper seeds last two years. By using proper techniques, the viability of pepper seeds can, however, be extended dramatically. The moisture content of the seed and the storage temperature are most important for the viability of the seed, and seed is best stored at low relative humidity and low temperature.

Drying the Seed

All extraneous pod material should be removed from the seeds, and damaged, discolored, or partial seeds should be culled. Ideally, pepper seeds should be dried to a moisture content of less than 8 percent. This is easily accomplished by drying the seed at 100°F for six hours. Spread the seed on trays and place it in an unlit gas oven, or outside in the shade if the temperature is high and the humidity is low. Never use a microwave oven to dry seed. Generally speaking, seeds that are hard and crunchy when they are bitten into are dry enough to store.

Storage

Any moistureproof container can be used to store seed, including sealed cans, jars, and even self-locking plastic bags. Take care that the containers are properly labeled for the variety of seed, and, obviously, never mix varieties in a container.

In Bethesda, Maryland, Howard Essl raises about 375 different varieties and grows out about ninety of those for seed. To store seeds, he places them in moistureproof barrier pouches with silica gel and then heat-seals the pouches. He claims that this technique maintains seed viability for up to twenty-five years.

The containers should be kept cool, so store the seeds in a refrigerator or freezer. Captain Charlie Ward of Virginia Beach, Virginia, says that his frozen seed remains viable for many years, but growers are advised to include moisture-absorbers such as silica gel if the seeds are to be frozen. When both seed moisture and storage temperature are low, longevity and germination are unaffected by the presence of oxygen.

CHAPTER 9

Harvest Time

 Back in the spring of 1989, Nancy Gerlach, who is a registered dietitian and the food editor of *Chile Pepper* magazine, wrote an article entitled "Too Many Peppers," in which she noted that a productive pepper garden is both a blessing and a challenge. "The blessing comes from the fact that fresh or freshly preserved peppers will be available year-round. The challenge comes from the sheer number of pods to be processed before they are lost forever." Nancy then went on to describe the various methods of preserving peppers, and we thank her for her hints. She closed the article by admitting: "Actually, there is no such thing as too many peppers, not as long as you have a variety of ways to preserve your abundance. If you plan your garden, you can make sure the varieties of peppers you harvest are versatile enough to be used fresh or preserved."

 Before we discuss harvesting, let us warn you about pepper burns—an occupational hazard. Burns on exposed skin from the capsaicinoids in hot peppers can be painful, so we recommend that anyone processing or chopping peppers of any kind wear rubber gloves. Despite such warnings, some people will, however, forget and burn their hands. If you have been handling peppers, do not touch sensitive parts of your body, your eyes or genitals, or they will be seriously burned. Remedies for burned hands call for plunging them into cooking oil or chlorine bleach, but the best treatment is to rub the burning area with isopropyl (rubbing) alcohol. Capsaicin is soluble in the alcohol and will be removed. Then rub an ointment such as Preparation H salve over the burned area.

The Art of Picking

About peppers, the question most commonly asked on the Gardening Bulletin Board of the Prodigy computer network is "When should I pick the pods?" The answer truly is: Whenever you want. Depending on geographical area, during the summer and fall there will be pods in every stage of development, from the recently pollinated to those that have dried on the bush. Because of the fruit-load restrictions (see chapter 6), it is important to harvest the maturing pods so that the pepper plant will continue to flower and produce fruit.

Judging Maturity

Check the descriptions in chapters 2 and 3 of the mature size of the pods in the different varieties. The simplest method is to feel the pod. If it is firm, it is ready to be picked. If it is soft, it is immature.

Although peppers can be picked at any stage of development, early pods have not had time to develop their full flavor or heat level. Usually, the first chile peppers available are the smaller varieties that are used green in fresh salsas—Piquins, Serranos, Jalapeños, and the young green pods of other types such as Habanero.

The larger pods of the Poblanos and the New Mexican varieties such as 'New Mexico 6-4', 'Sandía', and 'NuMex Big Jim' do not have to be peeled if they are finely minced before being used in a recipe that will not be cooked, such as a fresh salsa. The preferred method is to roast and peel them first (see page 187).

The best time to pick chiles for drying is when they just start to turn red—or brown in the case of 'Mulatos' and Pasillas. This timing will stimulate the plant into further production of flowers, and the harvested chiles can be strung to dry and will continue to turn the mature color. Pods allowed to dry on the bush will eventually either fall off, be partially eaten by birds or rodents, collect dust or dirt, or become discolored from ultraviolet sunlight.

Collecting the Pods

Choose pods that have smooth, shiny skins and are firm to the touch. A good rule to follow is that if the stem is easily detached from

9.1   Habaneros at the Perfect Stage for Picking

the plant, the pepper is ready. If it is necessary to tug on the pod, it is too early to pick it. If you are harvesting continuously to increase yield, it will be necessary to pick some peppers a bit early. When harvesting, it is best to cut the peppers off the plants with a knife or a pair of scissors because the branches are brittle and will often break before the stem of the pepper pod will.

The pepper-growing Penn brothers of Lago Vista, Texas, have invented an original technique for preserving whole fresh pods such as Habaneros. The pods are carefully washed and then submerged in honey. The honey prevents air from reaching the peppers and spoiling them, and the pods stay amazingly firm and fresh. The hotter varieties, such as Habaneros, also add heat and flavor to the honey. When needed for a fresh salsa, the pods are removed from the honey and washed off—and are hardly sweet at all. The only problem with this technique is that Habaneros (and other thin-walled pods) may be moldy on the inside of the pods and the mold is sometimes transferred to the honey. Cut a few pods open first to see if they have any mold before placing them in the honey.

Drying Peppers

Drying is the oldest and most common way to preserve pepper pods and works well for most peppers—except for the very meaty ones such as Jalapeños, which are smoke-dried and called *chipotles* (see page 185). To dry peppers, select those that have reached their mature colors, or are just starting to turn. If they are picked while still green, it is very likely that they will never turn the mature color. Avoid any pods that have black spots, because these will mold or rot. On dry days, the peppers can be placed on metal racks and set in the sun. Placing them on a surface that collects heat, such as a car hood or roof, accelerates the process. They can also be hung individually on a clothes line. Another method to use is a home dehydrator—just follow the manufacturer's instructions. Some of the larger growers use forced-convection solar dryers, which reduce the time needed for sun-drying by 65 percent.

Dehydration also works for fresh New Mexican or Ancho/Poblano peppers (either green or red), which are first roasted and peeled and then placed in the sun to dry. Lay long strips of the peeled pods on nylon window screening, cover them with cheesecloth, and place them in a semishady place with good air circulation. The more humid the climate, the more the drying pods should be exposed to the sun. This process makes *chile pasado* (literally, "chile of the past"), which will turn an unappetizing dark color, almost black. When the *chile pasado* is rehydrated in water for about thirty minutes, it regains its green or red color. One ounce of *chile pasado* is equivalent to ten or twelve fresh pods.

Ristras *and Wreaths*

The long red *ristras* (strings) of New Mexican chiles are seen everywhere in that state in the early fall. They provide decoration, but are also the centuries-old method of drying long red peppers for using later. To make a *ristra*, a supply of freshly picked, red (or just turning red) New Mexican chile pods is necessary; three-fourths of a bushel (approximately four pounds) of chiles will make a *ristra* about three feet long. Do not use green chiles in the hope that they will turn red. Many will be immature pods that will shrivel and merely turn a dull white. *Ristras* and wreaths can be made out of any elongated pods, so try making them with Cayennes or Mirasols.

Besides the pepper pods, a ball of lightweight cotton string and some baling wire or heavy twine is needed. The first step is to tie clusters of three pods together with the cotton string, or with rubber bands. Hold the three pods by their stems, wrap the string around the

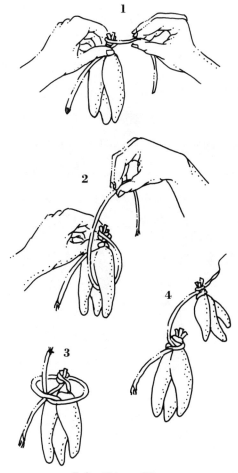

9.2 Tying a *Ristra*

stems twice, bring the string upward between two of the pods, and pull tight. Then make a half hitch with the string, place it over the stems, and pull tight.

Continue this process with sets of three pods until there are several clusters of pods tied to the cotton string, or until the weight of the pods makes the string difficult to handle. At that point break the string and start again, continuing until all of the pods have been tied into clusters of three.

The next step is to attach the clusters of pods to a stronger length of twine or wire. Suspend the twine or wire from a rafter or the top of a door and make a loop at the end to keep the chiles from slipping

9.3   Finished *Ristras*

off. Starting from the bottom, braid the pods around the twine as if braiding hair: The twine serves as one strand and two pods in the cluster serve as the other two strands. As the pods are braided, keep the center pushed down to insure a tight fit, and be sure that the pods protrude evenly from the *ristra*.

To make a wreath, use smaller pods, such as Cayennes, and braid the pods around a straightened-out coat hanger and then bend the wire into a circle. When the braiding is completed, hang the *ristra* or wreath in full sun from a clothesline or rafter where there is good air circulation. The chiles should dry in the sun before the *ristra* is brought inside or else they may turn moldy and rot. Do not spray the *ristra* with lacquer to make it shiny—all that will do is to make the peppers inedible. Dry red peppers have their own natural luster and do not need an artificial shine.

Dried whole pods can be reconstituted in a variety of ways. They can be roasted very lightly on a griddle, they can be fried in a little oil until they puff and reconstitute themselves slightly, or they can be soaked in hot water for between fifteen and twenty minutes.

Making Chile Powders

Although whole pods retain their color and flavor best, another way to store peppers is to grind them into powder. We have had success with many different varieties either ground separately, or combined according to pod color. To keep the colors pure, the pods should be dried and the seeds removed. A shortcut for drying pods that will be turned into powder immediately is to halve the fresh pods, remove the seeds, chop them coarsely, and then microwave small quantities on low power until most of the moisture is gone. Place these microwaved pepper pieces in a food dryer or in the sun until they break when bent. They can also be dried in a 200°F oven for between six and eight hours. Remember, however, that drying fresh peppers in the oven for long periods of time tends to darken them, and that they have a tendency to fade under full sun.

The next step is to grind the peppers into powder. Be sure to wear a paint mask for at least some protection against the pungent capsaicinoid-laced particles. Prepare to sneeze a lot. Using a food processor or a chopper/grinder, purée the dried pieces to the desired consistency of powder. They may be ground to a fine powder called *molido*, or coarsely ground with some of the seeds, which is called *quebrado*.

Adventurous gardeners can experiment, creating powders of specific colors. For example, collect the different varieties of green, yellow, orange, red, and brown chiles and separate them by color. The colored powders can then be combined with spices, to make "chili powder" for chili con carne, or to be stored. Another use for the powders is to turn them into green, yellow, orange, red, or brown chile pastes, by mixing them with cooking oils, some chopped garlic, and a little vinegar. The colors of the powders tend to be a bit dull, but they can be brightened by adding a few drops of appropriate food coloring when making the pastes.

Smoked Peppers

Many varieties of pepper pods can be smoked to preserve them. The most commonly smoked is the Jalapeño, which is generally considered too fleshy to be dried. (It can, however, be dried by using the microwave technique described above.) Smoked Jalapeños are called *chipotles*, and Americans who love their smoky taste and fiery bite have recently been hit with high prices and a scarcity of product. With prices for these smoked Jalapeños reaching fifteen dollars a pound wholesale, home growers yearn to smoke their own. But the Mexicans have been fairly secretive about their techniques, and none of the books on peppers describes home smoking. After a trip to Mexico, we have solved this mystery—but the process takes some dedication.

The Mexicans use a large pit with a rack to smoke-dry Jalapeños. The pit containing the source of heat is partially underground with a tunnel leading to the rack. The pods are placed on top of the rack where drafts of air pull the smoke up and over the pods. The Jalapeño pods can be left whole or seeded. The latter, more expensive, are called *capones*, or castrated ones.

It is possible to make *chipotles* in the backyard with a meat smoker or Weber-type barbecue with a lid. The grill should be washed to remove any particles of meat because any odor in the barbecue will give the pods an undesirable flavor. Ideally, the smoker or barbecue should be new and dedicated to smoking peppers.

The quality of homemade *chipotle* will depend on the maturity and quality of the pods, the moisture in the pods, the temperature of the smoke drying the pods, and the amount of time the peppers are exposed to the smoke and heat. The aroma of wood smoke will flavor the Jalapeños, so choose carefully what is to be burned. Branches from fruit trees, or other hardwoods such as hickory, oak, and pecan work superbly. Pecan is used extensively in parts of Mexico and in southern New Mexico to flavor *chipotles*. Do not be afraid to experiment with different woods.

The difference between the fresh weight of the peppers and the finished product is about ten to one, so it takes ten pounds of fresh Jalapeños to produce approximately one pound of *chipotles*. A pound of *chipotles* goes a long way: A single pod is usually enough to flavor a dish.

First, wash all the pods and discard any that have been damaged by insects, are bruised, or are soft. Remove the stems from the pods before placing them in a single layer on the grill rack. Start two small fires, one on each side of the grill with charcoal briquets. Keep the fires small and never expose the pods directly to the flames or they will dry unevenly or burn. The intention is to dry the pods slowly while flavoring them with smoke. Before placing it on the coals, soak the wood in water so that it will burn slowly and create more smoke. The barbecue vents should be opened only partially to allow a small amount of air to enter the barbecue, thus preventing the fires from burning too fast and creating too much heat.

Check the pods and the fires hourly and move the pods around, always keeping them away from the fires. It may take up to forty-eight hours to dry the pods completely. The pods will be hard, light in weight, and brown in color when dried. If necessary, let the fires burn through the night. After the pods have dried, remove them from the grill and let them cool. To preserve their flavor, place them in a self-locking plastic bag. Store them in a cool, dry place. If kept dry, the *chipotles* will last for between twelve and twenty-four months.

Roasting and Peeling the Pods

The Ancho/Poblano and New Mexican varieties have tough skins that are usually blistered and peeled before the peppers are used in recipes that require cooking. Blistering or roasting the pepper is the process of heating the fresh pods so that the transparent skin is separated from the meat of the pepper and can be removed. Stuart Hutson, a chile pepper grower in Mesilla, New Mexico, describes this process as: "Roasting the hides off them, not cooking them."

To roast and peel peppers, first cut a small slit in the pod close to the stem end so that the steam can escape. The pods can be placed on a baking sheet and put directly under the broiler, or on a screen on the top of a burner. They can also be plunged into hot cooking oil to loosen the skins, but that method is messy and not recommended. It is easier to use a barbecue. Place the pods on a charcoal grill about five or six inches from the coals, turning them often. Blisters will soon form, indicating that the skin is separating, but take care that the pods are blistered all over or they will not peel properly. Although the pods may burn slightly, do not let them blacken entirely or they will be overcooked and will be nearly impossible to peel. The idea is to use intense heat for short periods of time rather than low heat for a long time. During the charcoal-roasting process, the sugar and starch in the chile caramelize, imparting a "cooked" flavor. A rapid roasting

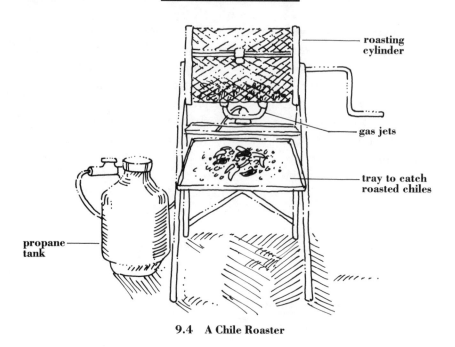

roasting
cylinder

gas jets

tray to catch
roasted chiles

propane
tank

9.4 A Chile Roaster

over high heat will leave the chile still tasting raw. During the roasting process, save a few perfectly formed pods and make a classic dish of *chiles rellenos*—stuffed peppers.

Remove the pods from the grill with tongs and immediately wrap the chiles in damp paper towels and place them in a plastic bag to steam for ten to fifteen minutes. For a crisper, less cooked pepper, plunge the pods into ice water to stop the cooking process.

Chile roasters have become commonplace in the Southwest over the past few years. These cylindrical cages with gas jets below can roast a forty-pound sack of chiles in less time than it takes to grill one pod over charcoal. The method is a more convenient way to process large quantities of pods, but there are some drawbacks to using a roaster. Occasionally the pods are roasted unevenly and some are difficult to peel. The pods are usually placed in a large plastic bag to steam after being roasted and must be processed as soon as they have cooled enough to handle. If allowed to sit for too long, bacteria growth can cause the pods to spoil.

Readers of *Chile Pepper* magazine have come up with some unusual methods for taking the skins off New Mexican chiles. One person wrote to say that he used a small propane torch to blister the pods one by one, and added that the flame can easily be directed into the creases. Perhaps the most unusual method was suggested by Chris Mathews of Marquette, Michigan. He wrote: "Freeze the little buggers solid. Using a dry rag to hold one end of the frozen pepper, use a vegetable peeler to peel the skin off, then a small knife or garnishing tool to scrape in the crevices the peeler missed."

Freezing Peppers

Peeled green pods can be frozen. If they are to be frozen whole (rather than chopped), the pods do not have to be peeled first. In fact, they are easier to peel after they have been frozen. Peel the pods only if they are to be frozen in strips or when chopped up.

Some sources call for blanching fresh peppers first, but in our experience, this step is not necessary. A handy way to put up chopped or diced chiles is to freeze them in plastic ice-cube trays. After they are frozen, they can be popped out of the trays and stored in a bag. When making a recipe calling for New Mexican chile pepper, just drop in a cube or two! This method eliminates the problem of trying to break apart a large slab of frozen chopped pods when you need only a couple of ounces.

The smaller fresh chile peppers such as Habaneros, Tabascos, Serranos, and Jalapeños can be frozen without processing. Wash the pods and dry them. Put them one-layer deep on a cookie sheet and flash freeze them. After they are frozen solid, store them in a bag. Bell peppers should be cut into strips before being frozen. Frozen peppers will keep for between nine months and a year at 0°F and will retain a surprising amount of texture. Few people can tell that the peppers, when chopped into a salsa, have been frozen.

Canning the *Capsicums*

The final authority on canning peppers is the New Mexico State Cooperative Extension Service, which developed the technique for the New Mexican varieties. We have followed their suggestions for canning. Because green chile is a low-acid fruit, we do not recommend that it be canned by itself. Can it with high-acid vegetables or liquids.

Chiles may be canned if you use a pressure cooker and *carefully* follow all the manufacturer's specific instructions. Roast and peel the peppers, remove the seeds, then wash and dry the pods. Pack them loosely in one-pint canning jars, leaving a one-inch head space. Add one-quarter teaspoon salt per pint jar and then add boiling water, again leaving a one-inch head space. Tighten the lids on the jars and place them in the pressure cooker. Place the lid on the pressure cooker, but let the steam escape for a full ten minutes before closing the petcock. Process pint jars for thirty-five minutes.

At the end of the processing, let the pressure fall to zero—that takes between twenty and twenty-five minutes. After opening the petcock, wait five minutes before opening the lid of the pressure cooker. The Extension Services suggest, as an additional safety precaution, that home-canned peppers be boiled for fifteen minutes before being eaten to prevent botulism poisoning. It is a lot less trouble to freeze the peppers rather than to can them!

Salsas and sauces may be canned in a pressure cooker, but the careful cook can use the water-bath method for these foods. Remember that peppers and tomatoes are both low-acid foods, so when you are using the water-bath method, the acid levels of the salsas must be increased by adding vinegar or lemon or lime juice to the mixture.

Pickled Peppers

Peppers can easily be pickled in a brine or a solution of vinegar and other seasonings, either by themselves or in combination with other vegetables. A peck maybe too many peppers to pickle, but a few jars will work out nicely. The various colors of peppers make attractive pickles, so mix and match such combinations as green Cayennes, orange Habaneros, red Serranos and Jalapeños, purple Ornamentals, 'Yellow Wax Hots', and even fresh red 'Thai' peppers.

A typical pickling recipe calls for pepper pods (with holes poked in them near the stem) and, optionally, mixed fresh vegetables such as broccoli, carrots, garlic, or pearl onions. Strips of larger peppers can be substituted for whole pods. The peppers and vegetables are placed in jars and covered with a solution of half water and half vinegar and one teaspoon of salt per pint of liquid. Spices, such as dill, can be added at this stage. The lids are then sealed tightly and the peppers should be left to pickle for about two or three weeks.

Nancy Gerlach offers some hints for pickling that should be followed no matter what recipes are used: Only use uniodized salt and *never* use a salt substitute; use a vinegar with an acetic acid content of between four and five percent; use distilled vinegar, not cider vinegar, which will discolor the peppers; and do not boil the vinegar for a long time as this will reduce the acidity.

Salsas and Sauces

Another way to use up a bumper crop of peppers is to make salsas and sauces and then freeze them. Numerous cookbooks have recipes for salsas (uncooked sauces), but the concept is simple. Peppers are chopped with tomatoes, onions, garlic, and spices such as fresh cilantro, parsley, or oregano. The usual proportion is two large tomatoes per onion, up to three garlic cloves, and peppers to taste, depending on heat level. The key to making good salsas is to hand-chop all ingredients; do not use a food processor. Ideally, salsas should be used fresh, but they can be frozen. The consistency will, however, suffer and the vegetables will not be as firm.

Cooked sauces freeze better than salsas do. Roasted and peeled New Mexican peppers are chopped coarsely and cooked with chopped onions, garlic, and a little oil for about thirty minutes. Then the sauce is cooled and frozen. Dried red New Mexican pods (or Anchos) can be softened in water, puréed in a blender, and then cooked with chopped onion and garlic for about an hour. The sauce is puréed again and then frozen. The gardener can use up a lot of pods by making sauces.

A sauce that does not use so many pods but is still fun is a traditional bottled hot sauce. Sometimes these hot sauces have vegetable bases, and sometimes they are all pepper. For a vegetable base, cook together in a little oil a half cup of chopped onions, the same quantity of carrots, and two minced cloves of garlic. When the vegetables are soft, purée them in a blender with five fresh peppers. Combine this mash with a half cup of vinegar and a fourth cup of lime juice and simmer for ten minutes. Strain the mixture into sterilized bottles and seal.

For a Louisiana-style hot sauce, take a pound of fresh red peppers, such as Tabascos or Serranos, and chop them coarsely. Combine them with two cups of vinegar and two teaspoons of salt and simmer for five minutes. Remove from the heat and purée the mixture in a blender. Let this mixture sit in the refrigerator for a couple of weeks, then strain it into sterilized bottles. To make Caribbean-style hot sauces, combine Habanero peppers with fruits such as papaya. Tamarinds are also commonly added to sauces in the islands.

The Challenge

Many other foods can be made to use up peppers. The pungent pods are commonly used in jams and jellies; Jalapeño jam is very popular, especially in Texas. Peppers are also combined with oils or vinegars to add heat and flavoring. One good combination we have tried is to steep tarragon and fresh *ají* chiles in vinegar for a few weeks, and then use the vinegar in salad dressings. Likewise, olive oil or any vegetable oil can be spiced up by steeping hot dried pods, such as Cayenne, in them. Other foods that can use up large numbers of peppers and then be stored are relishes, chutneys, mustards, butters, stews (such as red chile or green chile stew), and, of course, chili con carne.

If you still feel inundated by an overabundant harvest, give the pods away. Give them to neighbors or to family and friends all over the country as gifts. Trade them to restaurants that serve hot and spicy meals in return for a free dinner or two. (Many chefs have difficulty finding unusual varieties of fresh peppers.) Donate them to shelters for the homeless to spice up meals. Sell them at stands, flea markets, local grower's markets, or to specialty produce shops. Dry the pods and sell them by mail order with specific recipes designed for each variety.

CHAPTER 10

Growing Peppers Commercially

Although this book is designed for the home gardener, we felt it appropriate to include some information on growing peppers on a larger scale. An entire book could be written on commercial pepper growing—and probably will be some day. In the meantime, having studied some commercial pepper-growing operations in various parts of the United States, we will relate what we have learned. First, though, are the observations of coauthor Dave DeWitt, who once contemplated being a big-time chile pepper grower.

So You Want to Be a Pepper Farmer, Eh?

After a particularly good harvest, many of us amateur pepper gardeners yearn to go pro. We dream of hitting the big leagues and making a fortune by growing and harvesting the pungent pods. At the very least, we want to drive a big tractor.

Our fantasies are fueled by so-called friends who make inane comments, such as *"Dave, you're a pepper expert!"* (Note how they always speak in italics.) *"You could get rich growing Habaneros!"* (or whatever variety is currently fashionable).

Severely deranged by such comments, I recently decided to write a Business Plan for a Chile Pepper Farm. For readers who are not very knowledgeable about entrepreneurship, I should first point out that a Business Plan is phase one of starting a business; phase two is Sending Press Releases to the Media; and phase three is Declaring Bankruptcy.

Anyway, I began my Business Plan in a positive manner: "Net

10.1   New Mexican Chile Pepper Field

profit = $___ , ___ , ___ . __ ." Then I got stuck. I couldn't think of the number of dollars to fill into the blank, or even how to figure out the figure. So I showed my Business Plan to my friend Wayne, who gave me that special look he usually reserves for people who ask him for spare change.

"You schmuck," he said kindly (*schmuck* being the Urdu word for "balding, middle-aged dreamer"). "You can't estimate the net profit of a venture until you know your costs, the risk factors involved, the selling price of the goods. . . ."

"Don't confuse me with technical terms," I pleaded. "Just tell me where to start."

He gave a shrug and said, "So why not ask some chile pepper growers, already?"

"That's it!" I shouted in triumph. "Research!"

So I started my research by calling a noted chile pepper grower in the Mesilla Valley in New Mexico. For reasons of security and possible libel suits, I'll just call him "Joe." At first Joe was suspicious, apprehensive, and aloof. But after I offered him a $50/hour consultation fee, he became very helpful indeed.

"How many acres do you want to grow?" he asked.

I had no idea. How big is an acre, anyway? But I blurted: "A hundred!"

"Where's your land located?" he quizzed me.

Embarrassed, I replied, "Well, uh, you see, I don't, you know, really, uh, have the land. . . ."

"No problem," he said, "I'll lease it to you."

"You will? Gee, that's great. How much will that cost?"

"Just a hundred an acre per season," Joe said, but he was probably thinking, Hey, rube! Using my computerlike brain, I calculated that my expenses started at $10,000 just to lease the land.

"Then you'll need some seed," he suggested.

"Yeah, seed," I said. "Uh, how much seed?"

I could hear the sound of a calculator in the background as Joe said, "You'll need five to ten pounds per acre—figure an average of eight pounds per acre at $25 a pound, times a hundred acres. . . ."

"That's not too much?" I ventured.

"Nope," said Joe, "only about twenty grand."

I gulped. Now I was up to $30,000 in expenses and I hadn't even planted my first seed. "Okay, what next?"

"Of course, you have all the equipment?"

I didn't want to show my ignorance but I had no option. "What equipment?"

"I'd let you lease mine, but it's all tied up in onions."

"I'm making a shopping list," I told Joe. "Shoot."

"Tractor," he said. "About 105 to 120 horsepower."

"I've always wanted to drive one of those," I admitted. "How much?"

"Oh, about fifty to eighty grand, depending on options."

"Can I convert my Volvo?"

Joe chuckled. "Along with your new tractor, you'll also need a laser plane system with scraper and electronics, that's about thirty grand. You'll need a plow and a twelve-foot offset disker; together they're about thirteen thousand. Oh, and don't forget that four-row cultivator for about three grand."

"I'd never forget something as important as that," I promised. "Does it plant my seeds for me?"

"I'm getting the idea you've never grown peppers before," Joe said.

"Not true," I bristled. "I've had highly successful pepper gardens for over ten years. I've grown over thirty different varieties. . . ."

Joe guffawed. "Do you know about laser leveling?"

"Huh?"

Joe dissolved in hysterical laughter, then recovered briefly. "To insure proper drainage, you'll probably need a four-inch drop per acre. And surely you know about capping the seeds. . . ."

"Huh?" I could barely understand him as he explained between outbreaks of hysterics.

"You have to plant the seeds a foot deep in the bed to protect them from the cold—that's the cap. Then, after irrigating, precisely when the seeds are germinating, you have to scrape off that cap of dirt to within one-half inch of the seeds. If you miscalculate, you'll either leave the seeds too deep to sprout or scrape the seeds out of the bed and ruin your whole crop. Removing the cap at exactly the right time separates the men from the boys."

"Oh, no," I sobbed.

"It gets worse," Joe teased. "If you underirrigate, the plants will get blossom-end rot and the pods will be worthless. If you overirrigate, the plants will get phytophthora wilt and die."

"You mean die, like dead?"

"Yep."

I tried to regroup. "Let's not talk about the negative side of it," I pleaded. "Suppose I do everything right. How much money can I make? What's the bottom line?"

By now Joe had controlled his laughter to a mere chortle. "If you're lucky, you can gross about one and a half dry equivalent tons per acre, worth about $1,700."

"But that's $170,000 for a hundred acres," I chortled.

"Less up-front expenses," he pointed out.

I quickly calculated. "Uh, less expenses of $126,000 makes $44,000."

"You forgot fertilizer, labor, and harvesting costs," said Joe in a mocking tone.

"Arrrggghhh!" I screamed. "Why would anyone want to grow peppers?"

"It's a crop shoot," Joe admitted. "But if you know what you're doing and stick with it, you can eke out a living—assuming, of course, you don't lose your entire crop to the virus."

"Virus?" I mumbled, barely coherent by now. "Look Joe, I'll, uh, get back to you." Then I gently replaced the receiver and gave thanks to every god listed in *The Encyclopedia of World Religions* that I was only assembling a business plan and not actually starting a pepper farm.

After all this research, I've learned how to handle those friends who are so certain I'll be rolling in bucks by growing a hundred acres of Habaneros. "I've got the plan, the land, and the seeds," I tell them. "Have you got two hundred grand?" It never fails. They back away, mumbling something about all their reserve equity being tied up in nonconvertible debenture bonds and, besides, even if they could sell short and release the funds, the computer that writes the checks just crashed its hard drive and they'll have to write the check by hand and send it from New York, which could take months.

Commercial Bell Pepper Growing

With approximately two hundred thousand tons of Bell peppers being produced a year in the United States, it is obvious that quite a few farmers *are* successfully growing peppers, Dave DeWitt's "research" notwithstanding. We have surveyed methods used in large operations from North Carolina south to Florida and west to California, and we summarize them here.

Growing Cycles

Fresh Bell peppers are continuously available in the United States. In central California, planting begins in the first part of May, harvest begins in mid–August, and continues until late October. In southern California, peppers are planted between March and May and harvested from July through December. In Florida, planting occurs between 1 August and 15 March; harvest begins in mid–October and continues until 1 July. And there are imports from Mexico.

Cover Crops and Crop Rotation

In Georgia, wheat, oats, rye, or ryegrass are planted in the winter to protect the soil from water and wind erosion. To improve soil

10.2   Transplants in a Greenhouse

structure and to add plant nutrients when they decompose, these crops are plowed under at least two weeks before planting. In all states, peppers are rotated with other crops such as alfalfa or cotton, and no two Solanaceous crops (such as peppers and tomatoes) are grown successively. Farmers in North Carolina grow peppers in fields previously planted with corn, sorghum, or small grains.

Site Preparation

Well-drained soil is a prime factor for good Bell pepper production. Sandy loam is preferred in most areas, and salty or alkali soils are avoided, especially in California. Farmers in Georgia use windbreaks to prevent damage from blowing sand. In most of the South raised beds up to eight inches high are used to insure adequate drainage. Rows, either single or double, are formed on the raised beds. Fertilizers containing nitrogen and potassium are commonly applied before planting.

Planting

In California, both direct seeding and transplants are used. In north-central California, Henry Yamoaka uses transplants at the beginning of the season and then switches to direct seeding using specialized equipment. In Georgia and North Carolina, transplants are almost always used. They are grown in greenhouses and sometimes in plant beds, but most often in styrofoam flats or plastic cell packs in plant trays. In some areas, planting beds, either in greenhouses or open fields, are used to grow transplants. In California, about four ounces of seed produce the eight thousand to ten thousand transplants needed per acre. In the South, about twelve thousand to fifteen thousand plants per acre are grown.

After about eight weeks of growing in the greenhouse, moisture is withheld and the transplants are placed outside to harden off. They are then inspected and only healthy, well-hardened, disease-free transplants are selected for the field. Transplants are generally placed in the field by machine planters manned by workers.

In California, the plants are spaced between twelve and fourteen inches apart on single-row beds measuring between thirty and thirty-six inches from center to center, or spaced between sixteen and eighteen inches apart on double-row beds measuring forty inches from center to center. In the South, the plants are spaced between twelve and sixteen inches apart on rows spaced between thirty and sixty inches apart in North Carolina and between thirty-six and forty-two inches apart in Georgia. In the South, black plastic mulch is frequently used over the rows to speed up the crop and reduce weeds.

Irrigation

In the South, peppers typically require one to one and a half inches of water per week. In North Carolina, it is recommended that if no rain falls for about a week or ten days, it is time to irrigate. Trickle (drip) irrigation is common in all areas, and it is also used to apply about half of the needed fertilizer over the growing period. Overhead sprinklers, which also provide protection from frost, are set to deliver about an inch of water every four days. In California and Texas, furrow irrigation from ditches or wells is commonly used.

Fertilization

The amount of fertilizer applied varies with the previous cropping history, the soil type, the inherent fertility of the soil, and the planned yield. Alton Bailey, who grows peppers and produces seed, notes that nitrogen leaches out of the soil and needs to be replaced in some manner. He suggests that peppers should follow a nitrogen-fixing crop such as alfalfa. In an interview, he recounted some huge yields of New Mexican green chile that resulted when peppers were planted in fields on which alfalfa had been grown the previous year. Alton recommends that after the pepper plants are up, they be side-dressed with nitrogen to maintain a healthy, deep green color to the foliage. (He also suggests that not enough research has been done on the subject of the nitrogen needs of pepper plants.)

Southern coastal soils require between 120 and 180 pounds of nitrogen per acre; Piedmont soils only require between 50 and 80 pounds per acre. Phosphate requirements average between 100 and 200 pounds per acre, potash, between 100 and 300 pounds. Fertilizing before planting, commonly done in all regions, usually requires the use of all of the phosphate, most of the potash, and one-third to one-half of the nitrogen. Side-dressing, mostly with nitrogen, is done two to three weeks after transplanting and at two- to three-week intervals thereafter. On sandy soils in the South, appplications of 15-0-14 and 14-0-14 fertilizers have increased yields.

In California, fertilizer is applied at the rate of between 150 and 200 pounds of nitrogen and 20 pounds of phosphate per acre. Growers there stress that the nitrogen requirements depend on the particular field and are never the same from year to year. Experience and observations of the foliage determine when nitrogen is added and how much is applied.

Cultivation and Weeding

Farmers avoid using fields infested with perennial weeds such as Johnson grass and Bermuda grass, or annual weeds such as morning glory and Jimsonweed. In many areas, including the South, the mechanical rolling cultivators used for weed control and to oxygenate the soil are set very shallow (one inch) to avoid injuring the pepper roots. Herbicides, including Ambien, DcPA (Dacthal), and Devrinol, are commonly used, but all sources emphasize extreme caution and advise checking with extension agents before application. Plastic mulch will eliminate weeds on the ridges, but they still must be controlled in the furrows, and mechanical and hand weeding is effective for that.

Problems

Henry Yamaoka, who grows Bell peppers in California, says that his biggest problem is hot weather (temperatures over 90°F), which interferes with flowering and fruit-set. Blossom-drop from temperature and water stress is also a problem in the South. Blossom-end rot, from a calcium deficiency, is prevented by maintaining uniform moisture. It may also help to add lime to soil that is deficient in calcium. This is not a problem in most western states. Sunscald is a problem wherever the pods are exposed to the direct rays of the sun when the plants have lost their foliage prematurely because of stress, nitrogen deficiency, or bacterial leaf spot.

Bacterial leaf spot is the most serious disease of peppers in the South. Infected plant material and seeds are the main culprits. The seed can be treated by soaking it in a one-to-four solution of sodium hypochlorite under constant agitation for forty minutes. One gallon treats one pound of seed, which is then rinsed with vinegar and dried.

Southern stem blight, a fungal disease that causes wilting, is fought by burying crop residues and removing infected plants. Damping-off, the collapse of seedlings caused by two species of fungus, is often prevented if the seedbeds are fumigated. In Texas and California, phytophthora blight, which causes root rot, is a problem, especially where drainage is poor. Good cultural techniques and resistant varieties are being used to combat this fungal disease. Tobacco mosaic virus attacks peppers in North Carolina, especially in tobacco-growing areas. When possible, resistant varieties are planted to avoid the problem.

The most injurious insects for commercial Bell operations are cutworms, thrips, fruitworms, aphids, hornworms, borers, maggots, and weevils. Farmers scout insect infestations by taking field samples and by setting yellow sticky traps, black-light traps, and others to indicate the onset of infestation. In North Carolina, farmers have learned to prepare for the worst. Aphids, for example, are worst in mid-June, borers and earworms attack in early July, and borers, earworms, and armyworms reach devastating levels in early August. Insecticides are applied to fight the insects.

Harvesting

Peppers grown for the fresh market in the South are hand-picked by workers walking through the fields or riding on harvesting equipment. Yields average three hundred bushels per acre. The peppers are collected in buckets and dumped on a moving belt that takes them to a hopper. From the hoppers, they are transferred to twenty-bushel bulk bins. Then they are carried from the field to a central packing area where they are washed in a sodium hypochlorite solution, dried, sorted, sized, graded, and packed in cartons. Precooling with forced air at between 48°F and 50°F before shipping reduces rotting. For transport to market, the peppers are placed in well-ventilated shipping containers and then into refrigerated trucks. Extension bulletins from Georgia and North Carolina emphasize that truck refrigerators are not designed to cool the peppers down, but merely to maintain their existing temperature, so precooling is essential. Buyers will not accept warm peppers.

Costs and Profits

In North Carolina in 1988, total costs including harvesting but excluding plastic mulch, irrigation, grading, packing, and shipping were about $1,300 per acre, and the profit after expenses was approximately $1,200 per acre. The additional expenses of packing, shipping, and marketing would reduce that figure. In Georgia in 1990, the average cost per acre was $2,009, with an average profit of about $487 per acre.

A New Mexico Chile Pepper Operation

Jimmy Lytle comes from a pepper-growing background. His mother, June Rutherford, is one of the country's top producers of certified chile seed, and his father, the late Jim Lytle, had the 'NuMex Big Jim'

10.3   Jimmy and Jo Lytle

variety named after him. It is no wonder that Jimmy and Jo Lytle are involved in nearly every aspect of the pepper business.

Unlike many growers in New Mexico, the Lytles do not just grow and sell chile peppers to processors. Frustrated by what they consider the low prices paid by processors, they decided to produce and sell peppers on the fresh market—and to cover all possible stages of that business from growing to selling at retail. To accomplish this, the Lytles have three divisions in their operation: Lytle Farms is the growing end, Big Jim Produce is the wholesale operation, and Hatch Chile Express is the retail shop and mail-order business.

The entire system starts, of course, with growing. In a typical year the Lytles have 250 acres under cultivation, with most of that devoted to growing four New Mexican varieties: 'NuMex Big Jim', 'New Mexico 6-4', 'Sandía', and 'Española'. Smaller plots are devoted to Jalapeños, 'Yellow Wax Hots', Piquins, Ornamentals, Habaneros, and 'Guajillos'. All of these chiles are grown for the fresh market except the 'Guajillos', which are dried for whole pods. Some of the New

Mexican varieties are allowed to go red and are dried whole, but most are picked green.

The season begins in late winter when the fields are prepared for planting. The first step is called laser leveling (or planing). The Lytles use laser-directed equipment to maintain a grade of about .02 percent so that the field will drain properly. The field is plowed and ripped, and then 11-50-20 fertilizer is broadcast before planting. The ground is disked and built up into rows; Jimmy advises that no large clods should be present. The field is irrigated after the rows are made. A machine called a bed shaper forms the rows into beds, which are all uniform in height and width.

Around the first week in March planting begins and, to produce a staggered harvest, continues until the last week in April. The seed is dropped by machine on a ridge on top of the row, and then a six-inch cap of soil is placed over the top of the row to reduce water evaporation.

Jimmy inspects part of the field each day to check on the progress of germination. After the seeds sprout and reach the "crook" stage, the scary part begins. With a dragging harrow and a chain behind it, the cap of the soil over the germinated seeds is scraped off, leaving a mere one-quarter inch of soil on top of the seeds. Needless to say, if the harrow is too high, the cap will be too thick to allow the seedling to emerge. If the harrow is set too low, the seedlings will be scraped right out of the row.

"I get very nervous at this stage," says Jimmy.

After the seedlings sprout, Jimmy waits until they have six leaves before thinning them. His workers pluck out the excess seedlings, a tedious job, leaving two plants every ten to twelve inches. The two plants growing together tend to support each other during high winds. The rows are then cultivated to build soil up around the seedlings for additional support.

Two weeks after thinning, a sidedressing of 25 percent liquid nitrogen is applied to the rows. Irrigation depends on many factors: the size of the plants, the amount of solar radiation, the air temperature and humidity, and the presence (or lack of) thunderstorms in the area.

"You get an instinct about when to irrigate," Jimmy says. "It's usually about every ten days in Hatch."

During the growing season, Jimmy worries more about disease than about insects. He has experienced phytophthora and verticillium wilt and many viruses, but insects are not too much of a problem. He has had some trouble with leafhoppers, aphids, and thrips, but unless there is a severe outbreak, he does not use insecticides. It is his policy to keep all chemicals to an absolute minimum. Weeds are controlled by a combination of shallow cultivation and hand hoeing. There is one big problem that cannot be solved or controlled: hail. In 1991, scattered hailstorms descended on Lytle Farms and the result was catastrophic.

"We were wiped out," Jimmy recalls with a catch in his voice. "It was a total loss." But the Lytles have bounced back, mostly because of their diversification.

Harvesting of green chiles begins during the first week in August and continues until the first of October. The red chile harvest begins about 15 September and runs until the middle of December, depending on weather and night temperatures. All of the chiles are picked by hand. Jimmy has not experimented with any of the mechanical harvesters now available because for the fresh market he needs perfect, unmarked pods.

After the pods are picked, they are sent to the Big Jim Produce warehouse where they are sorted, bagged, put on pallets, shrink-wrapped, and shipped by refrigerated trucks (a thousand forty-pound sacks to the truck) to supermarkets all over the Southwest and West, including California. Jimmy can't grow enough green chiles to meet the demand of his clients, so he buys from other growers. There is enough margin in the fresh-market chiles to make a small profit for both the growers and the produce company.

Select chiles are sent to the Hatch Chile Express store, where they are sold at retail to customers who have them roasted on the spot in cylindrical drums. The store also sells other chile-related merchandise such as bottled salsas, T-shirts, refrigerator magnets, books, pottery, dishes, and mugs. Jo Lytle says that many people drive up from El Paso just to buy their green chiles in Hatch, which has the reputation of producing the finest chiles in the state—an honor vigorously contested by growers in Las Cruces, Deming, and Roswell.

Jimmy's primary advice to pepper growers is to use good seed. By good seed, Jimmy means certified seed that is guaranteed free from out-crossing so that the variety grows true. Seed with a good germination percentage is also important.

"There's no such thing as seed that's too good," he cautions, pointing out that cheap seed usually results in pods of every size and heat level in the fields, and most of them unsalable. Also important, he advises, are good cultural practices and keeping the farming techniques as natural as possible—which he admits is difficult in a large, commercial operation.

Growing Habaneros in Texas

Jeff Campbell discovered Habaneros in 1980, a full decade before they became the darling of American pepper consumers. He was in Terlingua, Texas, at the time, attending the big chili cook-off there, when he met a man who showed him some orange, lantern-shaped peppers that were reputedly the hottest in the world. Jeff tasted the pods, agreed that they were extremely hot, and asked where they came from.

"Belize," answered the man (Jeff forgets his name), who added that they were impossible to grow in the United States because the seeds would not germinate. When Jeff said he had a pepper farm in the Hill Country, the man gave Jeff all his seeds and wished him luck. Thus was born a unique pepper growing operation.

Jeff soon learned that the trick to germinating Habanero seeds was bottom heat and a warm greenhouse. In 1981, at his farm in Stonewall, he grew a few plants that he isolated from his other peppers—Jalapeños, Serranos, Tabascos, and some New Mexican varieties. Each year thereafter, he increased the number of Habaneros and eventually began selling them fresh and using them in his value-added products, such as salsas. The response from his customers was overwhelmingly positive, so Jeff continued to expand his Habanero production.

By 1992, of Jeff's eighteen acres of peppers, four were planted in Habaneros, and he had contracted with a friend to grow his Habanero seeds in isolation, two miles from any other peppers. He germinates and grows seedlings in March in his greenhouse, which he keeps quite warm.

"Habaneros are tropical plants and they like heat," he notes. That is why he delays setting out his transplants until the soil warms—long after the last frost, about mid-May. First he fertilizes the soil with phosphate. After the plot has been plowed and fashioned

10.4   Jeff Campbell

into ridges and furrows on top of raised beds, the transplants are planted by hand rather than by machine. They are spaced between four and ten inches apart because Jeff believes that planting them further apart wastes space. Immediately after planting, the ridges are side-dressed with a 13-13-13 fertilizer and side-dressed again after four weeks.

Jeff hopes that rainfall will supply enough water, but when there is a dry spell, he furrow-irrigates with well water. "If the leaves are wilted in the morning, I irrigate," he explains. "If the wilting occurs at midday in 100-degree temperatures, that's normal."

During the growing season, his Habaneros have few problems. Aphids he controls by spraying, but no other insects bother his Habaneros—although he has had weevils attack his Jalapeños. Even the deer, which have eaten his Tabasco plants to the ground, avoid the Habaneros entirely. Weeding is done by hand.

The plants set fruit well in the high humidity of the Hill Country, and after the first reaping, Jeff side-dresses the rows again. The Habaneros grow about three feet tall and each plant produces anywhere from 50 to 100 pods, which mature to an orange color. They are harvested continuously after they begin fruiting.

Jeff sells some pods fresh, dehydrates some (which he grinds into powder), and is experimenting with smoking them in the fashion of *chipotles*. But most of the pods are processed into other products, including a paste, several salsas, and even lollipops!

10.5 Hand-Harvesting Peppers

Although he has never calculated his profit per acre, Jeff says that his Habanero operation is very profitable and he intends to keep expanding the acreage. One reason for his profitability is that, like the Lytles, Jeff has a retail store where he sells his fresh peppers, as well as products made of them.

Profitability

Profitability varies widely in the pepper business, depending on contracts with processors, fresh-market prices, weather, disease and insect losses, and the use of the peppers in salsas and other products made by the growers. Generally speaking, peppers produce the highest profits from value-added products, fresh-market crops, and crops grown for processing, in that order. The lowest profits seem to be generated from red chiles that are sold dried.

In 1989, the Department of Agricultural Economics at the University of Arizona made an extensive study of the costs and profits of both green and red chile production in Cochise County. The study was so detailed that it even included the depreciation, interest, taxes, and insurance on farm machinery used.

For red chiles, the profit picture was quite poor. From initial plowing through disking in the residue after harvesting, total gross receipts per acre were a mere $975, and the operating costs were $1,507, resulting in a gross loss of $532. With the deduction of depreciation, interest, taxes, and general farm maintenance, the loss increased to $674 per acre.

The profit picture for green chiles was much better. Total gross receipts per acre for green chiles were $2,192.50. After the operating cost of $1,740.61 was subtracted, the gross profit per acre was $451.89. After the depreciation, interest, taxes, and general farm-maintenance costs were deducted, the net profit per acre was $313.69.

Because most green chiles in Arizona are sold to processors, the profitability of a pepper farm could be improved by selling the peppers on the fresh market or by developing value-added products. As with any business, there should be someone ready to buy the product before the farming project is begun. Growers are also advised to start small and discuss the project first with their county extension agent.

Worldwide Hot Pepper Production

Until recently, it has been very difficult to find accurate statistics on chile pepper production from the rest of the world. The problem has been caused by a combination of lax record keeping and the lack of government publication of such data. But in 1988, the Asian Vegetable Research and Development Center (the AVRDC) in Taipei, Taiwan, held an international conference on tomato and pepper production. The results of that conference, published as *Tomato and Pepper Production in the Tropics*, is now available and contains much valuable data on world production.

Included here is a table listing statistics compiled from reports given at the conference. The statistics are not perfect but are the best we have. They reflect only reported commercial operations and do not include small home farm plots. Some countries do not distinguish between fresh or dry chiles so assumptions have been made based on the varieties grown. Fresh, or green, production figures have been converted to dry equivalent tons at the ratio of 8 to 1.

The biggest statistical problems are closest to home: J. A. Laborde and E. Rendon-Poblete point out that "the statistics for [Mexican] peppers are not very reliable, because they are expressed in two different ways: as 'pungent' and 'nonpungent' or as 'dry and green peppers.' Current figures do not specify which peppers are included in which group." Thus, the Mexican figures may include Bell peppers but may not include the production of Tamaulipas State, where most Serranos are grown. However, chile pepper data from the National Chile Conference held at San Miguel de Allende in 1984 compare favorably to the figures provided by Laborde and Rendon-Poblete and do not include Bells. Yes, it's very confusing.

Readers should remember that yield depends to a certain extent on the varieties grown. Varieties with smaller pods will produce less weight per acre. Figures do not include Bell pepper production. The countries are ranked by total yield. Also, some notable chile pepper–producing countries, such as Burma, Pakistan, Peru, Bolivia, Bangladesh, Tanzania, and Hungary, were not included in the AVRDC study.

International Hot Pepper Production

Country	Year	Acreage (in Acres)	Yield (Dry Equiv. Tons)
India	1986	2,202,746	707,900
Mexico	1988	156,840	536,000
Indonesia	1986	498,940	387,000
China	1988	148,200	212,500
Korea	1986	326,331	202,841
Thailand	1985	143,652	116,501
U.S.A.	1988	31,201	49,921
Taiwan	1986	7,047	21,218
Malaysia	1985	2,848	13,836
Japan	1984	351	400

In the United States, some states do collect data on chile pepper production (New Mexico does; Arizona started again in 1992), others do not (Texas and Louisiana do not; California stopped in 1992). The U.S. Agricultural Census keeps data only on acreage, so figures for the United States are extrapolated from a number of sources for the years between 1978 and 1988.

Hot Pepper Production in the United States

State	Year	Acres Harvested
New Mexico	1992	36,000
California	1982	5,594
Texas	1982	1,980
Arizona	1987	357
Louisiana	1978	200

Seeds and Other Supplies

There is, of course, no single source for all the varieties of peppers described in this book. Following is a list of some companies that sell pepper seed. To list every possible source would be unwieldy. The omission of any specific seed company is regretted but does not imply that its product is any less favorable than that of the companies listed. Also listed are the addresses of suppliers of bulk seed for commercial growers, a source for heirloom seeds, and the address of the largest *Capsicum* seed collection in the United States, from which seeds can sometimes be begged. (Note: Some seed companies do not publish their phone numbers in their catalogs.)

Seed Companies

ALFREY SEEDS
P.O. Box 415
Knoxville, TN 37901

W. ATLEE BURPEE CO.
300 Park Avenue
Warminster, PA 18974

ENCHANTED SEEDS
P.O. Box 6087
Las Cruces, NM 88006
(505) 233-3033

GURNEY SEED & NURSERY CO.
110 Capitol Street
Yankton, SD 57079
(605) 665-1930

HARRIS SEEDS
P.O. Box 22960
Rochester, NY 14692
(716) 442-0410

HASTINGS SEEDSMAN
P.O. Box 115535
Atlanta, GA 30310
(800) 285-6580

HENRY FIELD'S SEED AND
 NURSERY CO.
415 North Burnett
Shenandoah, IA 51602
(605) 665-9391

High Altitude Gardens
P.O. Box 4619
Ketchum, ID 83340
(800) 874-7333

J. L. Hudson, Seedsman
P.O. Box 1058
Redwood City, CA 94064

Johnny's Selected Seeds
202 Foss Hill Road
Albion, ME 04910
(207) 437-4301

Liberty Seed Co.
P.O. Box 806
New Philadelphia, OH 44663

Native Seeds/SEARCH
2509 North Campbell Avenue,
  #325
Tucson, AZ 85719
(602) 327-9123

Nichols Garden Nursery
1190 North Pacific Highway
Albany, OR 97321
(503) 928-9280

Old Southwest Trading Co.
P.O. Box 7545
Albuquerque, NM 87194
(505) 836-0168

Park Seed
Cokesbury Road
Greenwood, SC 29647

The Pepper Gal
P.O. Box 12534
Lake Park, FL 33403

Pinetree Garden Seeds
Route 100
New Gloucester, ME 04260
(207) 926-3400

Plants of the Southwest
Agua Fria Route 6, Box 11A
Santa Fe, NM 87501
(505) 438-8888

Porter & Son, Seedsmen
P.O. Box 104
Stephenville, TX 76401

Redwood City Seed Co.
P.O. Box 361
Redwood City, CA 94064
(415) 325-SEED

Rocky Mountain Seed Co.
P.O. Box 5204
Denver, CO 80217

Seeds of Change
1364 Rufina Circle, #5
Santa Fe, NM 87501
(505) 983-8956

Seeds West
P.O. Box 1739
El Prado, NM 87529
(505) 758-7268

Shepherd's Garden Seeds
6116 Highway 9
Felton, CA 95018
(408) 335-6910

Sunrise Enterprises
P.O. Box 330058
West Hartford, CT 06133

Territorial Seed Co.
P.O. Box 157
Cottage Grove, OR 97424
(503) 942-9547

Tomato Grower's Supply Co.
P.O. Box 2237
Fort Myers, FL 33902
(813) 768-1119

Twilley Seed Co.
P.O. Box 65
Trevose, PA 19053
(800) 622-SEED

Westwind Seeds
2509 North Campbell, #139
Tucson, AZ 85719

Commercial Seed Sources

The following suppliers offer seed in bulk.

ENCHANTED SEEDS
P.O. Box 6087
Las Cruces, NM 88006
(505) 233-3033
Types: New Mexican, Ornamental, Jalapeño, Mirasol, Pasilla, Cherry, Bell, Habanero, *rocoto*, Tabasco, *ají*, Cayenne, Serrano

LIBERTY SEED CO.
P.O. Box 806,
New Philadelphia, OH 44663
Types: Bell, Cuban, Jalapeño, Cayenne, Wax, Ornamentals

PETOSEED CO.
P.O. Box 4206
Saticoy, CA 93004
(805) 647-1188
Types: Bell, Cherry, Squash, Wax, Pimiento, Cayenne, Ornamental, Jalapeño, Serrano, Cuban

ROGERS NK
P.O. Box 4188
Boise, ID 83711
Types: Various multicolored Bells, including 'Jupiter Bell', Jalapeños

Heirloom Seeds

SEED SAVERS EXCHANGE
Route 3, Box 239
Decorah, IA 52101
Dedicated to the preservation of heirloom seed varieties, including many *capsicums*. They publish an annual yearbook listing available varieties.

NATIVE SEEDS/SEARCH
2509 North Campbell Avenue, #325
Tucson, AZ 85719
A source of heirloom pepper varieties, mostly from the Southwest and Mexico.

Germ Plasm Bank

The U.S. Department of Agriculture Plant Introduction Station in Georgia has a vast, three-thousand-variety collection of *Capsicum* seeds. Gardeners interested in growing unusual peppers can petition the station for a few seeds of selected varieties. There is no guarantee that the station can or will supply the seed, but it is worth a try for dedicated gardeners. Contact Gil Lovell, USDA-ARS Plant Introduction Station, 1109 Experiment Street, Griffin, GA 30223-1797.

Other Supplies

Tools, equipment, fertilizers, biological controls, gifts, greenhouse supplies, and lighting may all be obtained by mail order.

THE COOK'S GARDEN
P.O. Box 535
Londonderry, VT 05148
(802) 824-3400

GARDENS ALIVE!
P.O. Box 149
Sunman, IN 47041
(812) 623-3800

GARDENER'S SUPPLY CO.
128 Intervale Road
Burlington, VT 05401
(800) 660-1700

HASTINGS SEEDSMAN
P.O. Box 115535
Atlanta, GA 30310
(800) 285-6580

A. H. HUMMERT CO.
2746 Chouteau Avenue
St. Louis, MO 63103
(800) 325-3055

HYDROFARM
3135 Kerner Boulevard
San Rafael, CA 94901
(800) 634-9999

A. M. LEONARD, INC.
P.O. Box 816
Piqua, OH 45356
(800) 543-8955

OLD SOUTHWEST TRADING
COMPANY
P.O. Box 7545
Albuquerque, NM 87194
(505) 836-0168

MELLINGER'S GARDEN CATALOG
2310 W. South Range Road
North Lima, OH 44452
(216) 549-9861

NEW EARTH INDOOR/OUTDOOR
GARDEN CENTER
4422 East Highway 44
Shepherdsville, KY 40165
(502) 543-5933

SEED SAVER
P.O. Box 2726
Idaho Falls, ID 83403
(208) 522-2224

TOMATO GROWER'S SUPPLY CO.
P.O. Box 2237
Fort Myers, FL 33902
(813) 768-1119

WORM'S WAY
3151 South Highway 446
Bloomington, IN 47401
(812) 331-0300

Glossary

adobo **sauce**	A tomato-based sauce used to can *chipotles*
ají	The South American term for the *baccatum* pepper species
annuum	A pepper species (meaning "annual"), including most of the common pod types, such as New Mexican, Jalapeño, Bell, and Wax
anther	The reproductive part of a flower that produces and contains pollen
anthracnose	A fungal disease affecting plants that is characterized by dark sunken lesions or black blisters
baccatum	A pepper species (meaning "berrylike") consisting of the South American peppers known as *ajís*
calyx	The external, usually green, part of a flower composed of little leaves called sepals
campanulate	Shaped like a bell
capones	Seeded (or "castrated") *chipotles*
capsaicinoids	Seven related compounds that cause the sensation of heat (pungency)
Capsicum	The pepper genus, from the Greek *kapto*, "to bite"
ceviche	A lime-marinated fish dish flavored with fresh chile peppers
chile pasado	Dehydrated green chile peppers that can be reconstituted with water and used in cooking

217

chiles rellenos	A classic dish of stuffed fresh chile peppers
chilipiquin	The Texas term for a wild variety of Piquins
chiltepin	A wild variety of Piquin peppers with spherical fruit
chinense	A pepper species (meaning "from China"), which includes the extremely hot Habaneros
chipotle	A smoke-dried Jalapeño pepper
chlorosis	A plant disease marked by the yellowing of stems and leaves
cold frame	An enclosed, unheated covered frame for growing and protecting seedlings in the spring
compost	A mixture consisting largely of decayed organic material that is used to fertilize and condition soil
corolla	Flower petals that make up the inner floral envelope
cotyledon	The first leaf to emerge from the embryo of a seed plant
cultivar	A cultivated plant variety
damping-off	A fungal disease, sometimes occurring in humid greenhouses, which causes the stem of a seedling to rot
deciduous	Falling off seasonally (as of leaves)
diazinon	An insecticide used to control insect pests that attack peppers
dicotamous	Describes a plant whose number of flowers doubles as it grows (first two, then four, then eight, etc.)
dieback	A plant condition in which peripheral parts are killed by parasites
emasculation	To remove the stamen of a flower during the process of artificial cross-pollination
filament	The part of the stamen that holds the anther
friable	Used to describe the condition of soil, it is something easily crumbled
frutescens	A pepper species (meaning "shrubby"), which includes the Tabascos
gamete	The sperm cell (pollen grain) or egg cell, which after fusion produces an embryo

Habanero   A popular pod type of the *Capsicum chinense* species, famous for having produced the hottest pepper ever measured

habit   Refers to a plant's characteristic mode of growth

harden-off   To make a seedling hardy enough to withstand transplanting outdoors, i.e., by leaving it outside during the day and gradually reducing watering

hot cap   A miniature, single-plant greenhouse made from wax paper or clear plastic

humus   The organic portion of soil that comes from partial decomposition of plant or animal matter

hydroponics   Growing plants without soil in a water culture

Jalapeño   A pod type of the *Capsicum annuum* species, this is the best-known chile pepper worldwide and the state pepper of Texas

lanceolate   Shape of leaves in which the end, and sometimes the base, tapers to a point

meristem culture   Producing new plants from the undifferentiated tissue of the growing point

***mole* sauce**   A spicy sauce made of chile peppers and unsweetened chocolate and served with meat or chicken

molido   Finely ground chile pepper powder

mosaic   A plant virus characterized by dark green or yellow-and-green mottling of stems and leaves

mulch   Any material (such as straw, plastic, or newspaper) applied over the soil surface to retard weed growth, conserve moisture, and maintain a uniform temperature

mycelium   A mass of interwoven filaments that form the body of a plant fungus

necrosis   Death of a localized area on a plant

nicotine sulfate   An insecticide for controlling insect pests that attack peppers

Ornamental   A type of pepper that is showy and colorful and used primarily for display rather than eating (although they are edible)

ovate	Shaped like an egg
ovule	A rudimentary seed containing the embryo sac before fertilization
pendant	Suspended; hanging down
pistil	The seed-bearing organ in a flower
pubescens	A pepper species (meaning "hairy"), which includes the South American *rocotos*
pubescent	Foliage covered with fine short hairs
quebrado	Ground chile pepper powder that contains the seeds
ristra	A long string of dried New Mexican chile peppers, used both for storage and decoration
rocoto	The South American term for the fruit of *Capsicum pubescens*
row cover	Small tunnel-shaped greenhouses that protect plants in rows from wind, cold, and snow
Scoville Heat Unit	A measure of pepper pungency, or heat, named after Wilbur Scoville; peppers range from 0 to about 300,000 Scoville Heat Units
Serrano	An enormously popular pod type of the *Capsicum annuum* species, used extensively in fresh salsas
shoulders	The part of the pepper pod that is nearest the calyx
Solanaceous	Relating to the nightshade family of plants
stamen	The organ of a flower that produces the pollen, or male gamete; its parts include the anther and the filament
stigma	The part of a flower that receives pollen grains for reproduction and on which germination takes place
thrips	Small to minute slender insects that feed destructively on plant sap
truncate	Shape of pods or leaves in which the ends are squared off
variegation	The presence of two or more colors in leaves, flowers, or stems

Bibliography

Allard, R. W. 1960. *Principles of Plant Breeding*. New York: John Wiley.

Andrews, Jean. 1984. *Peppers: The Domesticated Capsicums*. Austin: University of Texas Press.

Bailey, L. H., ed. 1930. *The Standard Cyclopedia of Horticulture*. New York: Macmillan.

Bessey, Paul. 1990. "Southern Arizonans Hot on the Trail of Chiles Find Crop is Good." *Arizona Daily Star*, 28 September, 1E.

Birkeland, C. J. 1987. "Plant Breeding as a Hobby." Circular 817, University of Illinois.

Black, Lowell, et al. 1991. *Pepper Diseases: A Field Guide*. Taipei, Taiwan: Asian Vegetable Research and Development Center.

Black, L. L., and L. H. Rolston. 1972. "Aphids Repelled and Virus Diseases Reduced in Peppers Planted on Aluminum Foil Mulch." *Phytopathology* 62: 747.

Bosland, Paul W. 1992. *Capsicum: A Comprehensive Bibliography*. Las Cruces, N. Mex.: The Chile Institute.

———. 1992. "The Chipotle Mystery—Solved at Last!" *Chile Pepper* 6 (no. 5): 46.

Bosland, Paul W., et al. 1989. *Capsicum Pepper Varieties and Classification*. Circular 530, New Mexico State University, Cooperative Extension Service, Las Cruces, N. Mex.

Bosland, Paul W., A. L. Bailey, and D. J. Cotter. 1991. *Growing Chiles in New Mexico*. Guide H-230, New Mexico State University, Cooperative Extension Service, Las Cruces, N. Mex.

Briggs, F. N., and P. F. Knowles. 1967. *Introduction to Plant Breeding*. New York: Reinhold.

Brookbank, George. 1988. *Desert Gardening*. Tucson, Ariz.: Fisher Books.

Brucher, Heinz. 1989. *Useful Plants of Neotropical Origin*. New York: Springer-Verlag.

Carr, A. 1980. *Rodale's Color Handbook of Garden Insects*. Emmaus, Pa.: Rodale Press.

Cheng, S. S. 1989. "The Use of *Capsicum chinense* as Sweet Pepper Cultivars and Sources for Gene Transfer." In *Tomato and Pepper Production in the Tropics*, ed. S. K. Green, 55 (Taipei, Taiwan: Asian Vegetable Research and Development Center).

Chioffi, Nancy, and Gretchen Mead. 1991. *Keeping the Harvest*. Pownal, Vt.: Storey Communications.

Cihacek, Larry. 1985. "Managing Saline Soils." Guide A-107, New Mexico State University, Cooperative Extension Service, Las Cruces, N.Mex.

Cochran, H. L. 1935. "Some Factors Which Influence the Germination of Pepper Seeds." *Journal of the American Society of Horticultural Science* 33: 477.

Conway, K. E., and L. S. Pickett. N.d. "Solar Heating (Solarization) of Soil in Garden Plots for Control of Soilborne Plant Diseases." Extension Facts No. 7640, Oklahoma State University.

Cook, Jim. 1986. "Practices to Speed Vegetable Growth in Wyoming's Climate." Bulletin B-684.6, University of Wyoming, Cooperative Extension Service.

Cotter, D. J. 1980. "A Review of Studies on Chile." Bulletin 673, New Mexico Agricultural Experiment Station, Las Cruces, N.Mex. April.

Courter, J. W., et al. 1984. *Growing Vegetable Transplants*. Circular 884, University of Illinois at Urbana-Champaign, Cooperative Extension Service, Ill.

Cox, Jeff. 1979. "Climate Control—The Key to Pepper Production." *Organic Gardening*, December, 30.

Creasy, Rosalind. 1990. "Chiles for Flavor." *Organic Gardening*, March, 32.

Dainello, Frank, and R. R. Heineman. 1982. "Antitranspirant Effects on Chile Pepper Production." Bulletin PR-4021, Texas Agricultural Experiment Station, College Station, Tex.

———. 1986. "Plant Arrangements and Seedling Establishment Techniques for Long Green Chile Pepper Production." Bulletin PR-4369, Texas Agricultural Experiment Station, College Station, Tex.

Dana, Michael N. 1986. "Soil Sampling for Homeowners." Pamphlet HO-71, Purdue University, Cooperative Extension Service.

Davidson, R. H., and W. F. Lyon. 1987. *Insect Pests of Farm, Garden, and Orchard*. New York: John Wiley.

DeWitt, Dave. 1990. "So You Want to Be a Chile Farmer, Eh?" *The Whole Chile Pepper* 4 (no. 2):17.

———. 1991. "The Ultimate Chile Patch, Part III: Capsicums in Containers." *Chile Pepper* 5 (no. 1):20.

———. 1991. "Yo Soy un Chiltepinero!" *Chile Pepper* 5 (no. 3):22.

———. 1991. "Chili Con Brio." *Countryside*, December, 70.

———. 1992. *Chile Peppers: A Selected Bibliography of the Capsicums*. Las Cruces, N.Mex.: The Chile Institute.

———. 1992. "Mystery Pods: The Ultimate Chile Patch, Part IV." *Chile Pepper* 6 (no. 2):28.

DeWitt, Dave, and Jeff Gerlach. 1989. "The Ultimate Chile Patch." *The Whole Chile Pepper* 3 (no. 2):14.

———. 1989. "If You Can't Stand the Heat . . . Don't Bring These Chiles Into Your Kitchen." *Harrowsmith*, November/December, 44.

———. 1990. "Chile Peppers: Growing Fire in the Garden." *Fine Gardening*, January/February, 54.

———. 1990. "The Ultimate Chile Patch Update." *The Whole Chile Pepper* 4 (no. 2):13.

DeWitt, Dave, and Nancy Gerlach. 1990. *The Whole Chile Pepper Book*. Boston: Little, Brown.

DeWitt, Dave, and Mary Jane Wilan. 1992. *The Food Lover's Handbook to the Southwest*. Rocklin, Calif.: Prima Publishing.

Dremann, Craig. 1983. *Growing Chili Peppers in California*. Redwood City, Calif.: Redwood Seed Co.

Editors of Sunset Books. 1963. *Basic Gardening Illustrated*. Menlo Park, Calif.: Sunset Books.

Edwards, R. L., and F. J. Sundstrom. 1987. "Afterripening and Harvesting Effects on Tabasco Pepper Seed Germination Performance." *HortScience* 22 (no. 3):473.

Ellis, R. H., et al. 1985. *Handbook of Seed Technology for Genebanks*. Rome: International Board for Plant Genetic Resources.

Eshbaugh, W. Hardy. 1983. *Genetic Resources of Capsicum.* Rome: International Board for Plant Genetic Resources.

Esparsen, Carolyn. 1985. "Chile: Some Hot Tips." *Santa Fe New Mexican,* 8 May.

Everett, T. H., ed. 1964. *The New Illustrated Encyclopedia of Gardening.* New York: Greystone Press.

Facciola, Stephen. 1990. *Cornucopia: A Sourcebook of Edible Plants.* Vista, Calif.: Kampong.

Farmer, Cap. 1991. "Blinded by the Light . . . Indoors." *Chile Pepper* 5 (no. 2):25.

Fehr, W. R., and H. H. Hadley. 1980. *Hybridization of Crop Plants.* Madison, Wis.: American Society of Agronomy and Crop Science Society of America.

Ficter, George S. 1966. *Insect Pests.* New York: Golden Press.

Garcia, F. 1908. "Chile Culture." Bulletin 67, College of Agricultural and Mechanical Arts, Agricultural Experiment Station, Las Cruces, N.Mex.

Gent, Martin P. N. 1989. "Row Covers to Produce Red or Yellow Peppers." Bulletin 870, Connecticut Agricultural Experiment Station, New Haven, Conn.

Gerlach, Nancy. 1989. "Too Many Peppers." *The Whole Chile Pepper* 3 (no. 2):26.

Gerson, Robert, and Shigemi Honman. 1978. "Emergence Response of the Pepper at Low Soil Temperature." *Euphytica* 27: 151.

Ghate, Suhas R., and Manjeet Chinnan. 1987. "Storage of Germinated Tomato and Pepper Seeds." *Journal of the American Society of Horticultural Science* 112 (no. 4):645.

Goodspeed, Jerry, and Larry Sagers. N.d. "Composting." Horticulture Fact Sheet FS-H10, Utah State University, Cooperative Extension Service.

Granbury, Darbie M., et al. 1990. *Commercial Pepper Production.* Bulletin 1027, University of Georgia, Cooperative Extension Service, Athens, Ga.

Greenleaf, Walter H. 1986. "Pepper Breeding." In *Breeding Vegetable Crops,* ed. by M. J. Bassett, Westport, Conn.: AVI Publishing.

Haddad, Nada. 1990. "Backyard Composting." University of New Hampshire, Cooperative Extension.

Hatch, Duane. N.d. "Soil Testing Guide for Home Gardens." Fact Sheet FS-H5, Utah State University, Cooperative Extension Service.

———. N.d. "Preparing Garden Soil." Fact Sheet FS-H1, Utah State University, Cooperative Extension Service.

Heiser, Charles B. 1969, 1987. *The Fascinating World of the Nightshades.* New York: Dover.

———. 1985. *Of Plants and People.* Norman, Okla.: University of Oklahoma Press.

Heiser, Charles B., and Paul G. Smith. 1953. "The Cultivated Capsicum Peppers." *Economic Botany* 7 (no. 3):214.

Hoagland, D. R., and D. I. Arnon. 1950. "The Water-Culture Method for Growing Plants Without Soil." Circular 347, California Agricultural Experiment Station.

Iowa State University, Cooperative Extension Service. 1991. "Composting Yard Waste." PM-683.

Kaiser, Samuel. 1935. "The Factors Governing Shape and Size in Capsicum Fruits; a Genetic and Developmental Analysis." *Bulletin of the Torrey Botanical Club* 62 (no. 8):433.

Kyte, L. 1983. *Plants for Test Tubes, An Introduction to Micropropagation.* Portland, Oreg.: Timber Press.

Johnson, Mae Martha. 1991. "Canning Green Chile." Guide E-308, New Mexico State University, Cooperative Extension Service, Las Cruces, N.Mex.

———. 1991. "Freezing Green Chile." Guide E-311, New Mexico State University, Cooperative Extension Service, Las Cruces, N.Mex.

Lafavore, Michael. 1983. "A Pepper Talk." *Organic Gardening* 31: 34.

Lagoe, Ray. 1992. "Chilly Chiles." *Chile Pepper* 5 (no. 2):34.

Lantz, Edith M. 1943. "Home Dehydration of Chili." *Journal of Home Economics* 35: 222.

Louisiana State University, Louisiana Cooperative Extension Service. 1991. "Your Compost Pile." Publication 2414.

Lyon, David. 1990. "Cool Nights and Chile Days." *National Gardening,* February, 26.

"Master Chile Gardeners." 1990. *The Whole Chile Pepper* 4 (no. 2):15.

McReady, John J., and Donald J. Cotter. 1987. "Preplant Seed Treatment Effects on Growth and Yield of Chile Pepper." *HortScience* 22 (no. 3):435.

Miller, Mark. 1991. *The Great Chile Book.* Berkeley, Calif.: Ten Speed Press.

Mitchell, Irene. 1983. "A Chile for Every Taste." *Organic Gardening* (June):64.

Monette, Stephen, and K. A. Stewart. 1987. "The Effect of a Windbreak and Mulch on the Growth and Yield of Pepper." *Canadian Journal of Plant Science* 67 (January):315.

Moore, Frank D., and John C. Hansen. 1974. "Suggestions for High Altitude Home Vegetable Gardens in Colorado." Pamphlet 158, Colorado State University, Cooperative Extension Service.

Morton, Julia F. 1976. *Herbs and Spices.* New York: Golden Publishing.

Naj, Amal. 1992. *Peppers: A Story of Hot Pursuits.* New York: Knopf.

Nickel, Judy. 1987. "Hot Fun in the Sun, or How to Make Chile Ristras." *Albuquerque Tribune,* 19 October, B-1.

Odland, M. L., and A. M. Porter. 1941. "A Study of the Natural Crossing in Peppers." *Proceedings of the American Society of Horticultural Science* 38: 585.

Ogden, Shepherd. 1992. "Pots & Plans." *National Gardening,* January/February, 46.

Perry, Leonard. N.d. "Organic Mulches." Bulletin GL-6, University of Vermont, Extension Service.

Pestle, Ray. N.d. "Plastic Mulch Facts." Bulletin GL-7, University of Vermont, Extension Service.

Pety, Edna, and Donald J. Cotter. 1984. *Growth of Long Green Chile Pepper Fruit.* Research Report 556, New Mexico State University, Agricultural Experiment Station, Las Cruces, N.Mex.

Pickersgill, Barbara. 1969. "The Domestication of Chili Peppers." In *The Domestication and Exploitation of Plants and Animals,* ed. P. J. Ucko and G. W. Dimbleby, 443. London: Duckworth.

———. 1969. "The Archaeological Record of Chili Peppers (Capsicum Spp.) and the Sequence of Plant Domestication in Peru." *American Antiquity* 34 (no. 1).

———. 1984. "Migration of Chili Peppers, Capsicum Spp. in the Americas." In *Pre-Columbian Plant Migration.* Cambridge, Mass.: Peabody Museum of Harvard.

Plotnikoff, David. 1991. "The Little Shop of Peppers." *San Jose Mercury News*, 10 October, 1D.

Porter, Wayne C., and William W. Etzel. 1982. "Effects of Aluminum-Painted and Black Polyethylene Mulches on Bell Pepper." *HortScience* 17 (no. 6):942.

Proulx, E. A. 1985. "Some Like Them Hot." *Horticulture*, January, 46.

Purseglove, J. W., et al. 1981. "Chillies: Capsicum spp." In *Spices*. London: Longman's.

Rast, A. B., and C. C. M. M. Stijger. 1987. "Disinfection of Pepper Seed with Different Strains of Capsicum Mosaic Virus by Trisodium Phosphate and Dry Heat Treatment." *Plant Pathology* 36: 583.

Rivas, M., et al. 1984. "Germination and Crop Development of Hot Pepper After Seed Priming." *HortScience* 19 (no. 2):279.

Rupp, Rebecca. 1987. *Blue Corn and Square Tomatoes*. Pownal, Vt.: Garden Way Publishing.

Ruttle, Jack. 1992. "Rubbish!" *National Gardening*, May/June, 38.

Sais, James R. 1991. "Make Your Own Compost." Guide H-110, New Mexico State University, Cooperative Extension Service, Las Cruces, N.Mex.

Sanders, D. C., et al. 1988. *Commercial Pepper Production in North Carolina*. Bulletin AG-387, North Carolina Extension Service, Raleigh, N.C.

Schoch, Paul G. 1972. "Effects of Shading on Structural Characteristics of the Leaf and Yield of Fruit in *Capsicum annuum* L." *Journal of the American Society for Horticultural Science* 97 (no. 4):461.

Schweid, Richard. 1989. *Hot Peppers*. Berkeley, Calif.: Ten Speed Press.

Shannon, E. 1984. *Identifying Chile Diseases*. Circular 511, New Mexico State University, Cooperative Extension Service, Las Cruces, N.Mex.

———. 1989. *Chile Disease Control*. Guide H-219, New Mexico State University, Cooperative Extension Service, Las Cruces, N.Mex.

Shaugnessy, Carol. 1991. "Confessions of a Pili-Pili Smuggler." *Chile Pepper* 5 (no. 1):24.

Sherf, A. F., and A. A. MacNab. 1986. "Pepper." In *Vegetable Diseases and Their Control*. New York: John Wiley.

Smith, Paul G., et al. 1987. "Horticultural Classification of Peppers Grown in the United States." *HortScience* 22 (no. 1):11.

Somos, András. 1984. *The Paprika*. Budapest: Akadémiai Kiadó.

Sundstrom, F. J., et al. 1987. "Effect of Seed Treatment and Planting Method on Tabasco Pepper." *Journal of the American Society of Horticultural Science* 112 (no. 4):641.

Taber, Henry G. 1989. "Gardening Soil Management." Pamphlet PM-820, Iowa State University, Cooperative Extension Service.

Tanksley, Steven D. 1984. "High Rates of Cross-Pollination in Chile Pepper." *HortScience* 19 (no. 4):580.

Tindall, Terry. N.d. "Improving Garden Soils." Pamphlet EC419, Utah State University, Cooperative Extension Service.

Tozer, Eliot. 1988. "Quest for Fire." *National Gardening*, May, 36.

Tracy, W. W. 1902. "A List of American Varieties of Peppers." Bulletin no. 6, U.S. Department of Agriculture, Bureau of Plant Industry, Washington, D.C.

U.S. Department of Agriculture. N.d. "Making and Using Compost." Fact Sheet 4-5-1. U.S. Department of Agriculture, Washington, D.C.

University of California, Division of Agricultural Sciences. 1976. *Growing Peppers in California*. Leaflet 2676. Davis, Calif.

Vietmeyer, Noel, ed. 1989. *Lost Crops of the Incas*. Washington, D.C.: National Academy Press.

Wade, James C., and Deborah Young. 1989. *Arizona Vegetable and Crop Budgets*. Bulletin no. 8911, University of Arizona, Cooperative Extension Service, Tucson, Ariz.

Watson, Howard. 1992. "Power Peppers." *National Gardening*, April, 60.

Wilson, Jim. 1991. "Pepper Partners." *National Gardening*, November/December, 30.

Yepson, R. B., ed. 1976. *Organic Plant Protection*. Emmaus, Pa.: Rodale Press.

Index

Horticultural practices and procedures are listed in SMALL CAPS.
Scientific and foreign names are listed in *italics*.
Names of pod types are Capitalized.
Cultivated varieties are listed in 'single quotes'.
Page references to illustrations are in *italics*.

Worth, Dick, 125
wreaths, 34, 184

X

Xanthomonas campestris pv. *vesicatoria* (bacterial spot), 136

Y

Yamaoka, Henry, 199, 201
'Yatsafusa', 36
'Yellow Squash Hot', 55
yield, of pepper plants, 120–21, 122–24